Edward Bond

BINGO

Scenes of money and death

EYRE METHUEN

LONDON

000 22114

First published 1974 by Eyre Methuen Ltd
11 New Fetter Lane, London EC4P 4EE
Reprinted 1975
© *1974 by Edward Bond*
Printed Offset Litho in Great Britain by
Cox & Wyman Ltd, Fakenham, Norfolk

ISBN 0 413 31840 0 (*Hardback*)
ISBN 0 413 31850 8 (*Paperback*)

LUTON SIXTH FORM COLLEGE

21. JUL. 1978		
21. MAR 1995		

This book is due for return on or before the last date shown above.

3123

For

Jane Howell

Contents

Bingo

INTRODUCTION

Shakespeare had two daughters. Susanna is buried near him under stone in the chancel of the parish church, Judith was buried under grass outside in the churchyard and her grave is lost. Perhaps that sums up the difference between them. Shakespeare's opinions about them aren't known, but it seemed to me that his daughters' lives might have reflected those opinions: Susanna social, well-married and affluent, and Judith obscure, over-shadowed by her sister, married late to the unsuccessful publican of The Cage and deserted in her old age. Perhaps being brought up under Shakespeare's incisive perception and judgement shaped the whole of their lives.

Judith is the only daughter in the play. I gave the more comforting and strengthening role that I think Susanna played in his life to an old woman servant. I did this for my own dramatic convenience. The old woman's son is a victim of Shakespeare's business world. By making her close to Shakespeare I had a bridge between the two elements of the play, but I kept what I think is the true psychological situation: one woman (Susanna, or in the play the old woman) was close to him, and another (Judith, and probably also his wife) was estranged.

I've done something similar with my account of the enclosure which involved Shakespeare. Combe represents several men, and the undertaking signed in the second scene by Combe and Shakespeare was in fact between Shakespeare and a representative of the enclosers called Replingham (though Combe confirmed it later). Shakespeare's last binge was with Jonson and Drayton. Only Jonson is shown in the play. I've also altered some dates. For example, Shakespeare's theatre was burned down in 1613 not 1616. I made all these changes for dramatic convenience. To

recreate in an audience the impact scattered events had on someone's life you often have to concentrate them. I mention all this
because I want to protect the play from petty criticism. It is based
on the material historical facts so far as they're known, and on
psychological truth so far as I know it. The consequences that
follow in the play follow from the facts, they're not polemical
inventions. Of course, I can't insist that my description of Shakespeare's death is true. I'm like a man who looks down from a
bridge at the place where an accident has happened. The road is
wet, there's a skid mark, the car's wrecked, and a dead man lies by
the road in a pool of blood. I can only put the various things
together and say what probably happened. Orthodox critics
usually assume that Shakespeare would have driven a car so well
that he'd never have an accident. My account rather flatters
Shakespeare. If he didn't end in the way shown in the play, then
he was a reactionary blimp or some other fool. The only more
charitable account is that he was unaware or senile. But I admit
that I'm not really interested in Shakespeare's true biography in
the way a historian might be. Part of the play is about the relationship between any writer and his society.

*

Shakespeare created Lear, who is the most radical of all social
critics. But Lear's insight is expressed as madness or hysteria.
Why? I suppose partly because that was the only coherent way it
could have been expressed at that time. Partly also because if you
understand so much about suffering and violence, the partiality
of authority, and the final innocence of all defenceless things, *and
yet* live in a time when you can do nothing about it – then you feel
the suffering you describe, and your writing mimics that suffering.
When you write on that level you must tell the truth. A lie makes
you the hangman's assistant. It betrays the victim and this is
intolerable – because you are mimicking the victim, and the most
important thing you know is the innocence you share with him.
So if you lie the world stops being sane, there is no justice to

condemn suffering, and no difference between guilt and innocence – and only the mad know how to live with so much despair. Art is always sane. It always insists on the truth, and tries to express the justice and order that are necessary to sanity but are usually destroyed by society. All imagination is political. It has the urgency of passion, the force of appetite, the self-authenticity of pain or happiness – imagination is a desire that *makes* an artist create. The truths of imagination are strictly determined and necessary. They aren't 'revealed' to artists, they have to work and train and learn so that they become skilled at discovering them. But every artist often feels that what he's created is 'right' and he's not free to alter it. It's life that in comparison seems arbitrary and random – because society is usually based on injustice or expediency but art is the expression of moral sanity. Philistinism is so shocking because it assumes that, on the contrary, creative imagination is arbitrary and random, a self-satisfying game, mere fantasy – instead of being vital to human development. And of course, what artists most frequently lack is enough of this creative imagination. Or perhaps they only play it down because they're told art is for the rich and intellectual, that science is work but art only luxury or play. Perhaps also because many people do in fact 'exist' without art. Well, they've only had to do so in modern industrial societies and that's one reason why these societies are stagnant and inhuman. And there are also artists who shut themselves up in private fantasies. What they create has to be interpreted by an extra-artistic language. Their verbal or graphic images have no force, it's as if a spectator had to look up every word or sign in a dictionary. But imagination isn't random fantasy. The artist's imagination connects him to his audience's world just as much as his knowledge does. Because Jane Austen's imagination was weaker than her knowledge she could avoid writing about the Napoleonic wars – except perhaps as one cause of her general fear of poverty. But as she needed to express the objective truth about her characters – that is her need for moral sanity – this deepened her creative imagination. In *Persuasion* she'd already started to write about the experience of poverty and not just her fear of it, and if she'd lived longer she might well have written about war. Writers who don't develop in this way become shut up in private fantasies, experiments in style, unrewarding obscurities – they become trivial and reactionary.

Shakespeare's plays show this need for sanity and its political expression, justice. But how did he live? His behaviour as a property-owner made him closer to Goneril than Lear. He supported and benefited from the Goneril-society – with its prisons, workhouses, whipping, starvation, mutilation, pulpit-hysteria and all the rest of it.

An example of this is his role in the Welcombe enclosure. A large part of his income came from rents (or tithes) paid on common fields at Welcombe near Stratford. Some important landowners wanted to enclose these fields – for the reasons given in the play – and there was a risk that the enclosure would affect Shakespeare's rents. He could side either with the landowners or with the poor who would lose their land and livelihood. He sided with the landowners. They gave him a guarantee against loss – and this is not a neutral document because it implies that should the people fighting the enclosers come to him for help he would refuse it. Well, the town did write to him for help and he did nothing. The struggle is quite well documented and there's no record of opposition from Shakespeare. He may have doubted that the enclosers would succeed, but at best this means he sat at home with his guarantee while others made the resistance that was the only way to stop them. They were stopped for a time. The fields were not finally enclosed till 1775.

Lear divided up his land at the beginning of the play, when he was arbitrary and unjust – not when he was shouting out his truths on the open common.

*

The subtitle is 'Scenes of money and death'. We live in a closed society where you need money to live. You earn it, borrow it, or steal it. Criminals, and hermits or drop-outs, depend on others who earn money – there's no greenwood to escape into any more, it's been cut down. We have no natural rights, only rights granted and protected by money. Money provides food, shelter, security, education, entertainment, the ground we walk on, the air we breathe, the bed we lie in. People come to think of these things as products of money, not of the earth or human relationships, and finally as the way of getting more money to get more things. Money has its own laws and conventions, and when you live by money you must live by these. To get money you must behave like money. I don't mean only that money creates certain attitudes or traits in people, it *forces* certain behaviour on them. Charity seems an argument against this, but in fact it proves it. If you have a lot of money you might give some of it to the poor, or some pictures to the nation. But you won't give all you have because then you'd have no reserve, no one would work for you for wages and so you couldn't collect more money. Your actions aren't finally controlled by human generosity (at best they're only prompted by that) but by your selfish need. The money you keep back isn't morally neutral – like enough clothes or food – because you use it to influence the lives of other people who are also trapped by money. We're wrong when we assume we're free to use money in human ways. When livelihood and dignity depend on money, human values are replaced by money values. Certainly that's what's happened in our commercial, technological society. Money destroys the effect of human values in our society because consumer demand can't grow fast enough to maintain profits and full employment while human values are effective. A consumer society depends on its members being avaricious, ostentatious, gluttonous, envious, wasteful, selfish and inhuman. Officially we teach morality but if we all became 'good' the economy would collapse. Affluent people can't afford ten commandments.

Money is an important social tool. It's the means of exchange and of accumulating the surplus necessary to create modern industry. But we've reached a point where money isn't used to remove poverty but to create and satisfy artificial needs so that consumption will maintain profits and industrial activity. Keynes said that to maintain effective demand in an economy it would be better to pay men for 'digging holes in the ground' rather than that they should be unemployed, but he added ironically that he presumed a 'sensible community' would find something more socially useful for them to do. Well, a lot of the trash we produce for civilized consumption is far more silly and dangerous than holes in the ground. And that's only concerned with keeping society running – the far more important and difficult work of making it more civilized is mostly ignored. We think we live in an age of science, but it's also an age of alchemy: we try to turn gold into human values.

*

It seems that sometimes people can be made to behave badly with frightening ease and rapidity, but it only seems so. Their awareness of human values doesn't simply vanish. People have faults and, as in all evolving species, weaknesses – but human values are the most enduring things we have, stronger than our rational minds. We have the need and right to protect ourselves and our families, and in a crisis we help those we know, not strangers – but it isn't easy for us to do this at others' expense or to make others suffer. It's difficult for human beings to be unkind, and unpleasant to be arrogant. There's always a reason for aggression, and the only effective weapon against it is to remove the cause. Fear is a lack of understanding, and the only way to remove it is by reason and reassurance. Even the hate that comes from fear and aggression begins as a passion for justice. That isn't a paradox. Why did Shylock ask for his enemy's flesh? Because his own had been spat on.

There are two main sorts of political aggression. The first is the aggression of the weak against the strong, the hungry against the over-fed. That's easy to understand. The strong are unjust, and to survive and get elementary rights many people are forced to act aggressively. The second aggression is of the strong against the weak. How can an American drop bombs on peasants in a jungle if, as I said, a sense of human values is part of his nature? It takes a lot of effort, years of false education and lies, indignity, shabby poverty, economic insecurity – or the insecurity of dishonest privilege – before men will do that. The ruling morality teaches them they are violent, dirty and destructive, that the only decent course open to civilized man is to act as his own gaoler, and that men in jungles are even worse because they're as savage as animals *and* as cunning as men – history proves it. So he drops bombs because he believes that if the peasant ever rowed a canoe across the Pacific and drove an ox cart over America till he came to his garden, he'd steal his vegetables and rape his grandmother – history proves it. And history like the Bible will prove anything.

An old fascist (or an old miser) is always bitter and cynical. Not because his conscience troubles him! – but because he lives in conflict with his fundamental sense of human values. Men can only be content when they live in peace and shared respect with other men. It seems odd to say these things in a century of fascism and brutality, but the world is unhappy and violent not because we're cursed with original sin *or* original aggression, but because it it is unjust. The world is not absurd, it is finally a place for men to be sane and rational in.

Of course demands for justice sometimes conflict. But the reason these conflicts are hard to resolve is that the 'judge' is often more guilty than the other parties. Most established social orders are not means of defending justice but of defending social injustice. That's why compromises inside a nation or between nations are difficult to get, and why law-and-order societies are morally responsible for the terrorism and crime they provoke.

*

I wrote *Bingo* because I think the contradictions in Shakespeare's life are similar to the contradictions in us. He was a 'corrupt seer' and we are a 'barbarous civilization'. Because of that our society could destroy itself. We believe in certain values but our society only works by destroying them, so that our daily lives are a denial of our hopes. That makes our world absurd and often it makes our own species hateful to us. Morality is reduced to surface details and trivialities. Is it so easy to live like that? Or aren't we surrounded by frustration and bitterness, cynicism and inefficiency, and an inner feeling of weakness that comes from knowing we waste our energy on things that finally can't satisfy us? That's true of all parts of our society, from the theatre of the absurd to the broken windows of a youth club. It's not so odd, then, to say that people are only happy when their lives are based on human values. *If* we survive we have only two possible futures. Firstly, as technological ants engineered from birth to fit into a rigid society. Or secondly, as people who live consistently by the values that are part of their nature.

*

You can't do much by deciding to be happier, saner or wiser. That partly depends on society, and you can only change your life by changing society and the role you have to play in it. If, for example, society encourages greed and yet is based on the poverty of other societies, you can understand that without any 'enlightenment'. What sort of society do we want? The earlier, simpler culture related closely to the land has gone, and not enough people remember its skills well enough to teach them – and anyway those skills were too simple to support the huge masses of people who've grown up in an industrial culture with a highly technological relationship to the environment. So we have to make sense of our technological culture and divorce it from rampant commercialism. A factory isn't bad in itself. It depends how many other factories there are, what they make and how they're organized. Finally the only way to answer these questions is for the people who work in the factories to answer them.

Some people still think workers are apes who'd swing round in trees all day if someone else didn't give them orders. They ask, how on earth could workers organize this mess? But the question is, how can we get out of the mess? That's why it's the *lack* of democracy that's so inefficient. Our problems can't be solved by more information, more control, more social engineering, more compulsion, more rewards, more expertise. Experts can only reshuffle the elements of the mess or add more elements. The faults of technology are probably political as much as technological, but what always happens is this: a mess isn't solved by removing its cause but by adding a new apparatus to contain or redistribute the mess, and then a new apparatus to deal with the new apparatus. (Transport is a perfect example of what happens.) There is no structural logic, no way of getting organizational simplicity, no real evolutionary discipline. Technology is a way of solving problems, but the *total technological culture* will break down from time to time, perhaps even more often than other cultures do, because there's no structural integration between its parts, and various technologies are always in conflict. There is chaos because machines and technology are given priority over people. The only way to get a workable simplicity is for people themselves to decide how they want to live and work and what sort of communities they want to be in. Then people will not be subordinated to more and more machines.

Politicians have talked about democracy for three hundred years and now people have come to expect it. The myth has gone out of state and authority, the social structure of authority doesn't impress or intimidate any more. You see, if someone's authority ultimately derives from god, *that* impresses. But an expert doesn't have that sort of moral charisma. There's no reason why *he* shouldn't work for *you*. Well, if no one believes in god any more how can he run the world efficiently? Most people no longer believe that if god's son came down to earth again he'd be better advised to send him to Eton. Most working people no longer believe there are other people who know better than they do how they should live and work. That doesn't mean that everything they will do is practical common sense; the essential thing about acting responsibly is to have responsibility. Then you learn from experience, you learn what you don't know and what education you need. And the time to take responsibility is when the people who've already got it can't make it work – and that's our situation now. Our problems won't vanish and we won't step straight into a rational society. But rational processes will be brought back into society and problems can be solved instead of being compounded. We have to choose a new purpose for society, a new culture. There *is* a counter-culture ready and it's been developing for hundreds of years: it is democracy.

Bibliographical Note

Most biographies of Shakespeare barely mention the Welcombe enclosure, but all the documents and a full commentary are given in *William Shakespeare* by E. K. Chambers (2 vols).

Bingo was first presented at the Northcott Theatre, Devon on 14 November 1973 with the following cast:

SHAKESPEARE	Bob Peck
OLD MAN	Paul Jesson
SON	David Howey
WILLIAM COMBE	David Roper
BEN JONSON	Rhys McConnochie
JEROME	Derek Fuke
WALLY	Martin Duncan
FIRST OLD WOMAN	Joanna Tope
JUDITH	Sue Cox
YOUNG WOMAN	Yvonne Edgell
JOAN	Margot Leicester
SECOND OLD WOMAN	Margot Leicester

Directed by Jane Howell and John Dove
Designed by Hayden Griffin
Lighting by Nick Chelton

PART ONE
One: Garden
Two: Garden
Three: Hill

PART TWO
Four: Inn
Five: Fields
Six: Room

There is an interval after Part One.

Warwickshire 1615 and 1616

Part One

ONE

Garden. A hedge runs across the top of the stage. Left, a passage-way opening through it. Far right, an opening with a low gate leading to the road. A bench. The house is unseen, off left.

Emptiness and silence. SHAKESPEARE *comes in. He carries a sheet of paper. He sits on the bench. He silently reads part of the paper. An* OLD MAN *comes through the gap in the hedge. He cuts the hedge with shears as he comes through and goes on cutting this side of the hedge. Silence.* JUDITH *comes out of the house left. The men don't react. The* OLD MAN *goes on cutting.*

JUDITH (*to* SHAKESPEARE). Isn't it cold for you? (*Slight pause.*) Mr Combe's here.

> SHAKESPEARE *nods.* JUDITH *looks round and then goes back into the house.* SHAKESPEARE *lets his hand hang down with the paper still in it. Silence.*

OLD MAN (*contentedly*). Last toime this year.

> *Silence. The* OLD MAN *goes on cutting. A* YOUNG WOMAN *comes along the road and stops at the gate. She smiles archly at the* OLD MAN.

YOUNG WOMAN. How yo' now?

> *The* OLD MAN *nods at* SHAKESPEARE. *The* YOUNG WOMAN *sees him.*

YOUNG WOMAN (*politely*). Nicet mornin', sir, thank the lord. (SHAKESPEARE *nods. The* YOUNG WOMAN *holds out her hand. A moment's silence.*) Just a little summat. Yo' yont notice.
OLD MAN. Where yo' from, gal?

YOUNG WOMAN. On my way through.

OLD MAN. Where to?

YOUNG WOMAN. My Bristol aunt. My people died lately. My aunt wed a farmer – they'll hev work for us. (*She turns to go.*) I yont be no trouble.

SHAKESPEARE. Stay, stay. (*She stops.*) You'd rather have money not food?

YOUNG WOMAN. Ah, that I would.

SHAKESPEARE *stands and goes out left to the house.*

YOUNG WOMAN. Hev he gone for authority?

The OLD MAN *smiles at her. He goes to the gate and opens it.*

YOUNG WOMAN. Is that all roight? (*Uncertainly.*) I yont know . . .

The OLD MAN *carefully pulls her through. He shuts the gate behind her with his foot. He glances round and then touches her breast.*

YOUNG WOMAN (*looks round, afraid*). Not here.

OLD MAN. Yo'm a beauty, gal. Let us feel.

YOUNG WOMAN. Got money, hev yo'?

OLD MAN. Wait back a the garden in that bit a orchard.

YOUNG WOMAN (*looks towards the house*). He . . . ?

OLD MAN. No one yont see down there. I got money. You go sharpish an' keep low. I'll be down by-n'by.

The YOUNG WOMAN *goes through the gap in the hedge. The* OLD MAN *picks up his shears and cuts the hedge.* SHAKESPEARE *comes from the house. He carries a purse.*

OLD MAN (*amused*). Her run.

SHAKESPEARE. Call her. She'll be out on the road.

The OLD MAN *goes slowly through the gate, still carrying the shears. He looks right and left, then calls.*

OLD MAN. Gal. (*He comes back through the gate.*) Her run.

SHAKESPEARE *puts the purse in his pocket. The* OLD MAN
starts cutting the hedge again. SHAKESPEARE *sits on the bench.*
Silence. The OLD MAN *laughs a little to himself, just loud*
enough to be heard. SHAKESPEARE *doesn't react.*

OLD MAN (*steps back and looks at the hedge*). She yont need lookin'
at till next spring.

SHAKESPEARE *doesn't react. The* OLD MAN *goes out through*
the gap. SHAKESPEARE *is alone. He sits on the bench. The*
paper is beside him. A chapel bell begins to peal. It is very close.
SHAKESPEARE *doesn't react. An* OLD WOMAN *comes from the*
house. She wears an apron.

OLD WOMAN. Where's Hubby? (SHAKESPEARE *shrugs. The*
OLD WOMAN *calls.*) Father. (*To* SHAKESPEARE.) His drink's
on table if – (*The bell stops.*) – yo' see him. (*She calls.*) Father.
(*To* SHAKESPEARE.) Mr Combe's in the house a-talkin t'
Judith. Yo' yont ought-a set out here. That's cold afore you
feel it this toime a year.

SHAKESPEARE. It's the last of the sun.

OLD WOMAN. So it may be. (*Slight pause.*) Mr Combe's come
arter the land. Mornin', business. If t'was yonythin' else he'd a
come on an evenin'. (SHAKESPEARE *doesn't react.*) There's
plenty a talk! Some say summat, some say summat else. (*Slight
pause.*) P'raps he'll tell yo' what he's up to. (*Slight pause.*)
People kip arksin' me hev I 'eard yonythin'. Yo'll be brought
in – you stand t'lose.

SHAKESPEARE. And your son.

OLD WOMAN. An' a lot a others. What'll yo' tell him?

SHAKESPEARE. Your son told you to question me.

OLD WOMAN. They've hed a meetin'. They thought I ought-a
arkst.

SHAKESPEARE. I don't know anything.

OLD WOMAN. What'll yo' do?

SHAKESPEARE. There's plenty of time.

OLD WOMAN. Start buildin' bridges when your feet git wet. If he shut they fields up he'll ruin whole families. They yont got a penny put by. My son say he like a speak t'yo' bout it. I told him t'look in this mornin'.

SHAKESPEARE. Did you.

OLD WOMAN. I thought yo'd want t' hear him out.

WILLIAM COMBE *comes through the house.*

SHAKESPEARE. Mornin', Will.

COMBE. Mornin'.

OLD WOMAN. Mornin', Mr Combe.

SHAKESPEARE *nods and the* OLD WOMAN *goes out right through the gate.*

COMBE. Nice garden. Your hobby, is it?

SHAKESPEARE. No. I weed a bit. I get tired. I planted the maples.

OLD WOMAN (*off, on the road*). Father.

COMBE. Quiet for you after London. You should take an interest in local affairs. We could get you on the town council.

SHAKESPEARE. No.

COMBE. Well, no use if you're not dedicated. You have to find time for it. Pity, though.

OLD WOMAN (*off*). Father.

COMBE. How's your wife?

SHAKESPEARE. Much the same.

COMBE. Well . . . sensible to sit here – if you know how to sit. Wears me out, of course. Been listening to gossip?

SHAKESPEARE. I've heard something.

COMBE. The gossip's true for once. There are over four hundred acres of common field out at Welcombe. They're owned by a group of farmers and a crowd of tenants. It's divided up into so many bits and pieces no one knows where they are. We can't farm the way we want – we all have to do what the bad farmers do.

SHAKESPEARE. We?

COMBE. Me – and two other big land owners. We're going to enclose – stake out new fields the size of all our old pieces put together and shut them up behind hedges and ditches. Then we can farm in our own way. Tenants with long leases will be reallocated new land. Squatters and small tenants on short leases will have to go: we shan't renew. That leaves you, and some others, who own rents on the land.

SHAKESPEARE. The rents. I bought my share years ago out of money I made by writing.

COMBE. All the farmers on the common fields pay you a rent based on their earnings – so any change affects you. Quite a large part of your regular income must come from that rent. A sound investment.

SHAKESPEARE. I wanted security. Is it true that when you enclose you're going over from corn to sheep?

COMBE. Mostly. Sheep prices are lower than corn prices but they still give the best return. Low on labour costs! No ploughing, sowing, harvesting, threshing, carting – just a few old shepherds who can turn their hand to butchery. Sheep are pure profit.

SHAKESPEARE. But you know I could lose? I've got no labour costs, I just draw my rents.

The OLD WOMAN *comes through the gate. She crosses the garden and goes out left.*

COMBE (*factually*). Everyone listens to money. (*He looks off left a moment and then turns back to* SHAKESPEARE.) There's another problem: the town council also own some of the rents. They use their share to feed the town poor – seven hundred – not counting gypsies and riff-raff passing through. You see there's a lot of money involved!

SHAKESPEARE. The town will oppose you. A lot of the small holders don't have written leases. They just followed their fathers onto the land – and their fathers had followed *their*

fathers. If you get rid of them and the short-lease tenants –
there'll be more than seven hundred poor to feed. And if you
grow less wheat the price of bread will go up –

COMBE. Then it'll be profitable to grow more wheat and the
price will come down. Always take the long view, Will. I sel-
fishly cut down my labour costs and put up prices and the town
suffers – but not in the long run. This is the only way men have
so far discovered of running the world. Men are donkeys, they
need carrots and sticks. All the other ways: they come down to
bigger sticks. But there's a difference between us and the beast.
We understand the nature of carrots and sticks. That's why
we can get rid of the bad farmers who *grow* starvation in their
fields like a crop, and create seven hundred poor in a town of
less than two thousand. But – in the meantime the town council
will oppose me. They don't want to feed the new poor while
they wait for history to catch up with the facts. They're writing
to you for help.

SHAKESPEARE. Who told you –

COMBE. My friends on the council. You're one of the biggest
rent holders. You're respectable. They probably think you've
got friends in London. You could make out a strong case against
me.

SHAKESPEARE. We've come to the river.

COMBE. We needn't build a bridge if there's a ford down-
stream. Will you reach an agreement with me?

SHAKESPEARE. You'll get increased profits – you can afford to
guarantee me against loss. And the town councillors.

COMBE. I make all the effort, I expect to keep my carrot.

SHAKESPEARE. I invested a lot of money.

COMBE. I'll tell you why I'm here: I'll guarantee *you* against
loss, in return for an understanding.

SHAKESPEARE. Yes?

COMBE. Don't support the town or the tenants. When the council
write, ignore them. Be noncommittal or say you think nothing
will come of it. Stay in your garden. I'll pay for that.

SHAKESPEARE. You read too much into it. I'm protecting my own interests. Not supporting you, or fighting the town.

COMBE. That's all I want. It needn't be written into our agreement, it wouldn't read well: but it will be implied. After all, if we sign an agreement it wouldn't pay you to attack me: you get your present rents guaranteed at no extra cost. Free insurance. It pays to sit in a garden.

SHAKESPEARE. You guarantee me the difference between what my rents are now and what they'll be after enclosure, if they fall. How do we agree the figures?

COMBE. O, you can accept my –

SHAKESPEARE (*gives* COMBE *his sheet of paper*). I want security. I can't provide for the future again. My father went bankrupt when he was old. Too easy going.

COMBE (*holding the paper*). Yes, a nice man, but as you say, too . . . Very well. We'll appoint independent assessors. How many?

SHAKESPEARE. Another thing. I've got over a hundred acres of my own land out there. Are you after that?

COMBE. No, no. We won't touch your private land. This only affects your rents from the common fields.

> The OLD MAN *hurries in through the gap in the hedge. He is frightened but defiant, excited and amused. He looks round, backs a few steps towards the hedge and stands there.* SHAKESPEARE *and* COMBE *don't notice him.* COMBE *reads* SHAKESPEARE'S *piece of paper. A moment's silence. The* SON *comes angrily through the gap in the hedge. He is excited and tightjawed. The* SON *stares at the* OLD MAN *before bursting out.*

SON. Beast.

OLD MAN (*laughs briefly*). Look at him.

SON. Animal. In daylight. Back on a public high road. Any child could put its yead cross the wall.

> COMBE *stands up.*

OLD MAN (*pointing at the* SON). Look at him!

SON. Grey hair. Waggin' your boney ol' arse. Slobberin' like a boy with mud pies.

COMBE. He's got a woman in there.

SON. Hev yo' no shame? God an' man see you in the daylight. Yo'm drag creation down t' the beast. Animal. They ugly ol' legs. Runnin' loike a thief. Ugly.

JUDITH *and the* OLD WOMAN *come out of the house.*

Look at him! Where your wife an' child can see yo'.

JUDITH. What is it?

OLD WOMAN. Father, your drink's inside on the table.

OLD MAN. Yont sendin' me indoor. Look how red he go!

COMBE (*goes to the hedge and calls through*). Girl! Come here.

SON. Git her out. Thass her. Runnin' round them trees. Tried a climb the wall. I shut the gate on 'em when I saw what t'was. (*He goes to the gap and calls through.*) Come out. (*He turns to the* OLD MAN.) Loike an animal. Ugly. (*To the others.*) He yont hed the shame t'cover her yead with her skart.

COMBE (*calls*). You won't get out there. It's locked.

Silence. The YOUNG WOMAN *comes through the gap in the hedge.*

You're not a local girl.

YOUNG WOMAN. On my way t'Bristol, sir.

COMBE. Got work there?

YOUNG WOMAN (*nods*). Can I go, sir?

COMBE. No doubt your family's dead and your husband's left you?

YOUNG WOMAN. Not wed, sir. My family's dead though. Can I go?

COMBE. Who've you got in Bristol – your sister, uncle?

OLD MAN (*laughs*). Her auntie. Mr Combe almost got 'an roight.

COMBE. Dear me, we're in a bad way. Half the country's suddenly bereaved and they're marching round England to stay with relatives who live as far away as possible. The law says you can't leave your parish without a pass. Where's your pass?

YOUNG WOMAN. I yont no beggar woman, sir.

SON. Mr Combe's on the bench. Yo' hed it now. Yo'll be punished.

SHAKESPEARE (*to the* SON). Why were you in my orchard?

They all turn to look at SHAKESPEARE.

SON. I come t'see yo'. Mother say I . . .

The YOUNG WOMAN *starts to cry. They all turn back to her.*

YOUNG WOMAN. My aunt's waitin' in Bristol. My family's dead.

JUDITH. Where?

YOUNG WOMAN. Coventry.

JUDITH. Could you point out their graves?

YOUNG WOMAN. They'm buried in poor ground. Nothin' t'show.

COMBE. We have her sort in front of us every week, Judith. Do anything for money – though they'd rather do nothing. Lie when they learn to speak. First time they say father it's a lie. (*He laughs shortly.*) The law says you're to be whipped here in the shopping place till the blood runs and then sent back to your parish in Coventry, was it?

YOUNG WOMAN. Yont whip us, sir? I were whip afore an' that hurt my yead sorely. I couldn't go with people arter. I walked okkard an' fell down in the road. I were a gal then an' that's only better now.

COMBE. If there's something wrong with your head it'll do it good. Doctors whip mad people. I'd like to follow my own inclinations and let you off but I have to protect the public. You're a healthy girl, sleeping rough hardens your skin. You'll be all right. If you lead your sort of life you must learn to pay for it. (*To the* SON.) Take her to the lock-up.

The SON *starts to take the* YOUNG WOMAN *out.*

YOUNG WOMAN (*earnestly, not crying*). Yo' yont whip us, sir. That destroy my yead. The Constable's wife long a 'cester say that's a shame t'whip me. (*The* SON *takes her out through the gate. She is heard off on the road.*) I fall over the road, sir. Yont whip us.

COMBE. Tch, locusts or the blight. (*To* SHAKESPEARE.) I'll show this paper to my lawyers and be in touch. Goodbye.

COMBE *goes out left.* JUDITH *goes with him.*

OLD MAN. He git cross!

OLD WOMAN. Father, go in an hev your drink.

The OLD MAN *goes into the house.*

I'm sorry my boy shouted. Young people yont got no patience – worse'n us. I hope he yont upsit his father.

SHAKESPEARE. They're going to enclose.

OLD WOMAN. What'll you do?

SHAKESPEARE. Wait and see.

OLD WOMAN. Yo' give him a sheet a piper.

SHAKESPEARE. Nothing's decided. Has this shouting woken my wife? See if she's all right.

The OLD WOMAN *goes out left.* SHAKESPEARE *sits on the bench. He stares in front of him for a moment.*

TWO

Garden. Six months later.

The OLD WOMAN *and* JUDITH *are sitting alone on the bench.*

JUDITH. Has your marriage been happy?

OLD WOMAN. 'Twas. We had seven good year first off. Then the press men come t' church one Sunday mornin' an' hid back a the tomb stones. When the men come from the lord's supper out they jump an' tak em over sea t'fight. I still think a them times on an off. Time 'fore the flood.

JUDITH. Seven years out of a life. Most people don't have that.

OLD WOMAN. He were gone three year. Then two men bot him hwome. He'd bin hit top the yead with an axe. Some man were killin' a man lay on the ground front on him an' when he swung his axe back he hit father top the yead. Not the sharp end, though. That'd a kill 'un. Now he hev the mind of a twelve year ol' an' the needs on a man. I'm mother an' wife to him.

JUDITH. He should be happy. No responsibilities. No duties.

OLD WOMAN. He's a boy that remember what's like t'be a man. He still hev a proper feelin' for his pride, that yont gone. Hard, that is – like bein' tied up to a clown. Some nights he come hwome an' cry all hours. I git on with my work now. You hear him all over the house. Every room. An' the garden.

JUDITH. It was harder for your son. He had a child for a father.

SHAKESPEARE *comes out of the house.*

OLD WOMAN. No coat?

SHAKESPEARE. Is it cold? It looked warm from the house.

The OLD WOMAN *stands and goes off left into the house.*

JUDITH. Have you been up to mother?

SHAKESPEARE. What?

JUDITH. Shall we carry her down? The spring weather will help her.

SHAKESPEARE. She's happy in her room.

JUDITH. When are you going back to London?

SHAKESPEARE. I don't know.

JUDITH. I thought you were buying some property at Blackfriars.

SHAKESPEARE. That's done.

The OLD WOMAN *comes from the house with a wrap. She drapes* SHAKESPEARE.

SHAKESPEARE (*irritated*). Don't fuss!

> SHAKESPEARE *pulls the coat off and pushes it back to the* OLD WOMAN.

OLD WOMAN. I'll leave it there.

> *The* OLD WOMAN *puts the wrap on the bench and goes off into the house.*

JUDITH. Aren't you going away at all this year?

SHAKESPEARE (*still irritated*). I don't know.

JUDITH. Have you told mother?

SHAKESPEARE. She's not interested.

JUDITH. You'll get old sitting there all day.

SHAKESPEARE. I *am* old.

JUDITH. You used to be so busy. Striding about. Laughing. It's all gone. You look so tired these days.

SHAKESPEARE. I didn't sleep last night. So many people on the streets. All that shouting. And the sky – like day.

JUDITH. Someone's starting the fires. Everyone says so.

SHAKESPEARE. I'll put buckets on the stairs and by the doors. You must keep them filled. Thank god we're not thatched.

JUDITH. Why don't you tip the watch and tell them to keep an eye on us?

SHAKESPEARE. I have.

> *Silence.* JUDITH *looks at* SHAKESPEARE. *Then she gets up and goes silently into the house.* SHAKESPEARE *is alone. He leans back and slightly to one side with his head up and his hands in his lap. He closes his eyes. Silence. The* OLD MAN *comes silently through the gap in the hedge. A pair of shears hangs from his hand. He pays no attention to* SHAKESPEARE. *He stops and feels along the side of the hedge with the flat of his hand, as if he was blind. Then he begins to cut. Suddenly* SHAKESPEARE *notices him. He is shocked – but he doesn't make a sound or move violently.*

SHAKESPEARE. How long have you been there?

OLD MAN. Juss cuttin' back the young growth. That need air t' thicken out. Hev I woke you up then? Your daughter bin rowin', that it? Yont want a take no woman-row. Yo' got a fist. Thass only two piece a man's anatomy a woman understan', an' a fist's one. She yont hold with yo' set there all day.

> *The* YOUNG WOMAN *comes to the gate. The* OLD MAN *looks at her, goes to the gate, opens it. She comes in quickly and stands close to the hedge.*

SHAKESPEARE (*looks at the* YOUNG WOMAN. *There's a slight pause before he knows her.*) They sent you home.

OLD MAN. Her yont got no hwome. Her go back there her'll get whip again. So her run for it.

SHAKESPEARE. You mustn't walk in the streets. You'll be recognized.

YOUNG WOMAN. I mostly come out a night. I were frightid by meself t'day. I were clever, mind. When someone got by I stoop down an' do as though I brushin' my skart.

SHAKESPEARE. Where d'you live?

YOUNG WOMAN. Barns. They ol' burned 'ouses.

SHAKESPEARE. You're shaking.

YOUNG WOMAN. Ah, I do shake an' all! I bin took so since they whip us. I warned 'em straight. (*She shrugs.*) I yont feel cold but my arms an' legs do shake an' my teeth go a-clatter. (*She holds out her fore-arm.*) Yo' look, see 'ow the skin go in that arm, like a bud peckin'.

SHAKESPEARE. How did you get through the winter?

OLD MAN. I fed her.

YOUNG WOMAN. Sometime. I yont allus count on that. Sometime the boys come a-lookin' for us in they empty houses. Not s'much now. They say I have a sickness. I tell 'em I'm whole, thass only the whippin'. But they only come when they'm drunk. You yont heard a no cure for shakin'?

SHAKESPEARE. No.

YOUNG WOMAN. I cover meself proper but I still shakes. I try holdin' me yand tight. I set in the heat of a fire. But I still shakes. An' when that's cold the same. Well, there. I yont thrid needles for a livin'. I can larn t'live with it. Least it yont touch my yead.

SHAKESPEARE. You give her bread and lie with her.

OLD MAN. She's a poor creature. But us still hev some fun.

YOUNG WOMAN. O ah, us's allus laughin'.

SHAKESPEARE. At what?

OLD MAN. O – people?

YOUNG WOMAN. What they put on t' wear.

OLD MAN. They hats!

YOUNG WOMAN. An' what they say.

OLD MAN. Try t' tell yo' yo' yont know your own name.

YOUNG WOMAN. Gallopin' arter this an' that – but they mustn't pant! 'Howdedo.'

OLD MAN. 'Howdedo.'

The OLD MAN *and the* YOUNG WOMAN *laugh.*

YOUNG WOMAN. Us laugh so us hev t' cover us yeads –
OLD MAN. So us yont git caught.

The OLD MAN *and* YOUNG WOMAN *laugh.*

YOUNG WOMAN. Well. (*She holds out her hand.*)
SHAKESPEARE (*calls*). House!

The YOUNG WOMAN *runs towards the gate.*

OLD MAN. Don't frit. He'll give yo' proper fettles sit out on a table like a christian.

JUDITH *comes out of the house.*

SHAKESPEARE. Let her eat. Give her a shawl or a dress. Both. Give her your mother's things. They're only gathering dust.

JUDITH (*unsure*). I know her. (*She recognizes her.*) She – . (*To* SHAKESPEARE.) No. If we feed her once we'll never get rid of her.

YOUNG WOMAN. That's roight enough. Give us some money an'
I'll away t' go. I yont need feedin'.

SHAKESPEARE. She must be looked after.

JUDITH. She'd steal if we had her here, the poor thing.

YOUNG WOMAN. Missis is roight. It yont do t'trust me. Give us a
bit a money. Yont notice that.

The bell starts to peal.

JUDITH (*to the* OLD MAN). D'you often have her in the garden?

OLD MAN. No.

JUDITH. How often?

SHAKESPEARE *sits on the bench.*

SHAKESPEARE (*to the* YOUNG WOMAN). Wait in the orchard till
it's dark. Then go away. (*To* JUDITH.) Give her some money.
No, bring my purse.

YOUNG WOMAN (*looks at the gap in the hedge and hesitates*). I
yont go down there agin–

SHAKESPEARE. The back gate's locked now.

The YOUNG WOMAN *goes through the gap in the hedge.*

JUDITH. Why is she so frightened?

SHAKESPEARE. She shakes because she was whipped.

JUDITH *goes left into the house.*

OLD MAN. Now she's cross with the two on us. My boy's cross
too. He rage up an' down all hours. Say yo' agin poor people.
Ol' Combe tak the best land, an' do he give yo' any that yont
be good enough t' grow stones in. (*He shrugs.*) I tell 'im yo'
live a rare ol' life but there's no harm in yo'. He's allus talkin'
t'god – so stands t' reason he never listen to a word I say.

SHAKESPEARE. Why is your son afraid of the devil? God judges,
not the devil.

OLD MAN. When my boy's took in a hoolerin'-bout he say the
devil look arter his own.

SHAKESPEARE. By putting them in the fire? You never sell every-thing. That's what he punishes. Hell is full of burning scruples.

The OLD WOMAN *comes out of the house.*

OLD WOMAN. Mr Combe.

SHAKESPEARE *nods.*

OLD WOMAN. (*to the* OLD MAN). Let the gen'men talk, father.

The OLD WOMAN *goes into the house. The* OLD MAN *takes another cut at the hedge and then follows her.* SHAKESPEARE *sits alone for a moment. He raises his head as* COMBE *comes out of the house.* COMBE *carries a bottle of ink, a pen and a document.*

COMBE. In your garden? The day for it. I haven't seen you since winter. Busy. (*He puts the pen and ink on the bench and hands the document to* SHAKESPEARE.) From my lawyer. (SHAKESPEARE *starts to read the document.*) Pity you didn't go into business before. You can bargain. That guarantees you against any loss arising from my action.

SHAKESPEARE. You'll enclose?

COMBE. My men start digging – (*The bell stops.*) – round my my land on Monday. I've signed it.

SHAKESPEARE (*reading the document.*) Bells love silence.

SHAKESPEARE *signs the document.* COMBE *picks it up and looks at it.*

COMBE. I'll have it witnessed. Must keep you on good behaviour, living by the chapel.

JUDITH *comes out of the house.*

JUDITH. Mr Combe – I thought it was! How is Mrs Combe? (*She shakes* COMBE's *hand.*) . . . No. I won't have it. (*Icily cold.*) Father, where is he? It's shameful.

SHAKESPEARE. No.

JUDITH (*icy*). Don't shield them. You're morally as guilty as they are.

COMBE. What is it?

JUDITH. Our garden man. In that hedge.

COMBE (*amused*). With a woman? (*He goes to the hedge and looks through the gap. Then he looks back at* SHAKESPEARE.) I know why you like your garden!

> COMBE *goes out through the gap in the hedge.*

JUDITH. I'm sorry, father, I will not allow that woman – (*She points left to the house.*) – to be abused. How can you behave so badly? It's irresponsible! Why d'you make it necessary for a child to speak to its parents in this way?

> *The* YOUNG WOMAN *runs through the gap in the hedge, over the garden and out through the gate.*

How sordid. Ugly. (*She stares angrily after the* YOUNG WOMAN *But doesn't try to stop her. She is still like ice.*) On one's own property.

> JUDITH *goes to the gate and shuts it.* COMBE *walks through the gap in the hedge. He is still amused.*

COMBE. Gone?

JUDITH. Yes. Thank you.

COMBE. She was hiding behind the trees. Bolted like a rabbit when I said boo. I had a clear sight of her. (*He turns to* JUDITH.) There was no one with her.

SHAKESPEARE. She wants work. I told her she could work in the scullery.

COMBE. No, she can't. She was sent away from here to her proper parish, and she's come back. Tch. The lord chancellor's told the benches they aren't firm enough. Well, I am. I'll have the barns and burned houses searched. I know where they lie up. (*He goes towards the gate.*) The law says it's an offence to give alms to anyone without a licence. So don't be tempted.

Goodbye. I'll get my men on to her. She won't make herself a nuisance anymore.

COMBE *goes out through the gate.*

JUDITH. Last time they . . . So of course I thought . . .

SHAKESPEARE. I came out here to rest. People coming and going. (*He sighs.*) Haven't you any work in the house?

JUDITH. How could I let him enjoy himself while his wife . . .? She's had a hard life, father. You don't notice these things. You must learn that people have feelings. They suffer. Life almost breaks them. (*She picks up the pen and ink.*) I'll take these in. You don't need them? You sit there and brood all day. People in this town aren't so easily impressed, you know. We can all sit and think. (SHAKESPEARE *is silent.*) I feel guilty if I dare to talk about anything that matters. I should shut up now – or ask if it's good gardening weather. D'you know why mother's ill? D'you care?

SHAKESPEARE. Judith.

JUDITH. At last, a word. I'll tell you why she stays in bed. She hides from you. She doesn't know who she is, or what she's supposed to do, or who she married. She's bewildered – like so many of us!

SHAKESPEARE (*flatly*). Stop it, Judith. You speak so badly. Such banalities. So stale and ugly.

JUDITH. I can only use the words I know.

The OLD WOMAN *and the* OLD MAN *come out of the house left. She wears her outdoor coat. He carries the basket.*

OLD WOMAN. We'm away now. There's nothin we'm forgot?

SHAKESPEARE (*to the* OLD MAN). Combe found her.

OLD WOMAN. Oh dear.

JUDITH (*to the* OLD WOMAN). That girl was –

OLD WOMAN. Hubby told me. Us were goin' t'put her up for a few days, now I know on it. Then p'raps summat could be worked out. Surely there's summat?

SHAKESPEARE. Combe's men are looking for her. ˙

> *The* OLD MAN *sits on the bench. He rests his elbows on his knees and his hands hang down between his legs. He rocks like a little boy. The basket is on the ground beside him.*

JUDITH. They'll flog her! O, why wasn't I more careful? You all think I should be in her place. (*To* SHAKESPEARE.) You could have warned me! You ignore me – you always do! You talk to the servants more than to your family.

OLD MAN. That's worse'n that. She lit they fires. I yont know why. She wait up in they empty houses till that's dark then out she go an' back she come an' set down in the corner. She yont tell but I knew what t'was. Her face blacked up an' she smelt of smoke. Smell it for days.

OLD WOMAN. No one else know.

OLD MAN. They'll find out. When they lock her up. Her'll tell.

OLD WOMAN. You're not t' fault. Us won't let em touch you.

OLD MAN. They'll hang her. (*He starts to cry.*) O dear, I do hate a hanging. People runnin' through the streets laughin an' sportin'. Buyin' an' sellin'. I allus enjoyed the hangings when I were a boy. Now I can't abide 'em. They conjurors with red noses takin' animals out the air an' coloured things out their pockets. The soldier lads scare us. The parson an' 'is antics.

OLD WOMAN. Mr Shakespeare yont like yo' cryin in his garden. (*She helps the* OLD MAN *to his feet.*) I'll manage the basket. (*To* JUDITH.) Goodbye then. He'll be round for work in the mornin'. (*To the* OLD MAN.) We'll soon be hwome. (*To others.*) I'll git him t'bed early.

OLD MAN (*crying as he goes*). People pushin' t'see in they empty coffins. Allus so quiet fore the rope go so's yo' hear babbies an dogs cry – an' when it thump the people holla.

> *The* OLD MAN *and the* OLD WOMAN *go through the gate.*

OLD WOMAN (*out on the road*). Hush now. I hev a noice surprise indoor for yo', my lad.

OLD MAN (*out on the road*). That better be good.

OLD WOMAN. That's good. I hid un so yo'll hev t' find it first.

The OLD MAN *and the* OLD WOMAN *go away down the road.*

JUDITH. I can't leave you out here. It's against common humanity. You'ld better come inside and learn to put up with us.

SHAKESPEARE. Go in.

JUDITH. You'll catch cold and expect to be nursed. I've enough to do with mother on my hands. Why are you so stubborn. Your family's tearing itself to bits and you sit in the garden and –

SHAKESPEARE. Yes, yes.

JUDITH. Yes, yes – it's easy to make us sound stupid. You ignore the people you share a house with and when they try to talk, you sneer.

SHAKESPEARE *goes out through the gate.* JUDITH *follows him onto the road. She can be heard calling after him.*

If we bore you why don't you go away, father? Go back to your interesting friends. Or are they tired of you now?

THREE

Hill. A pleasant warm day. Slight fresh wind. The YOUNG WOMAN *has been gibbeted. An upright post with two short beams forming a narrow cleft. The* YOUNG WOMAN's *head is in this and her body is suspended against the post. A sack is wrapped round her from hips to ankles. A rope is wound round the sack and the top half of her body to steady her against the post. (Rembrandt, New York Metropolitan Museum of Art, inv. 76487. 'Rembrandt's Drawings' Schedig, W. Ill. 121.) She has been dead one day. The face is grey, the eyes closed and the hair has become whispy.*

A bench downstage left. SHAKESPEARE *sits on it facing away from the body, out into the audience. He is alone.*

Two labourers come in. Both middle aged. They watch the body for a moment.

JOAN (*reflectively*). By roights they ought- a put her on a bonfire, for lightin' fires. Or starve her in a cage for beggary.

JEROME. Set yo'self down, gal'. I'm tired.

They sit on the ground, unpack their lunch and eat.

JOAN (*quietly as she points to* SHAKESPEARE). Is the gen'man all roight?

JEROME (*nods and eats*). Gen'man from big 'ouse: New Place gen'man.

They eat in silence for a moment.

Good.

JOAN. Like it?

JEROME (*nods and eats*). Good stuff.

JOAN. Take some a mine.

JEROME. No, gal.

JOAN. Go on, I offered, yo' yont arkst.

JEROME. Yont yo' 'ungry?

JOAN. I got extra. I know hot weather allus give yo' an appetite.

JEROME. Yo' pick your grub like a bud with a wart end on its beak. (*He puts his arm round her waist.*)

JOAN. Hold your noise, boy. An' give over throwin' crumbs down the front a my dress. (*She takes his arm from her waist, uncorks a bottle and gives it to him.*) Grab hold a that. Yo' need two hand a feed yo'self.

JEROME (*drinking*). Yo'm a hard woman.

JOAN (*eating*). So'd yo' be if yo' kip gettin' crumbs down the front a your dress. (*She takes crumbs from her bodice and feeds the birds.*) Cheep-cheep, chuck-chuck, my beauties.

The SON *comes on with* WALLY. WALLY *is tall and quite thin.*

SON. Mornin', brother, sister.

WALLY. Morn'. (*He stares at* JOAN *and* JEROME.)

JOAN. We'm on us way t' work. Stonin' our strip a field out at Welcombe. We'm just cooched-ed up for us bit a fitter.

JEROME (*eating*). Which we'm earnt. Sorry yont none left t' hand round. (*He drinks.*)

JOAN. Hev yo' see her drop? (WALLY *shakes his head.*) Proper state her were in. Yont heard a word parson say, poor chap. But she went good as gold.

JEROME (*eating*). He say up yo' git, my gal, an' up she git.

JOAN. Tryin' a help 'em hang her. (*She finds more crumbs in her bodice.*) Cheep-cheep. How the wicked disguise themselves. Her could a bunt the town t'death. When her toime come she couldn't hold a candle straight t' see where she were goin'. She die summat slow. No family or friends t' swing on her legs. I sin mothers an' fathers help their young a go easy afore. She yont afford a pay the hangman t' do it.

SON. A festival a dark. Singin', dancin', layin' money how long she'll live. The sexes going back a hedges. Is that reverence? Lord god is wherever there's justice. When a soul go satan-ways lord god come t'watch an' weep. Reverence, friends. That ought-a be a festival a light an' prayer.

JOAN (*quietly. Feeding birds*). Chuck, chuck, chuck.

WALLY. P'raps they'm makin' a great show for the presence a lord god, brother. Soundin' the psalter an the joyful harp.

SON. You'm too good natured, brother. Let us talk with lord god.

The SON *and* WALLY *shut their eyes and clasp their hands. They don't kneel.* JOAN *bows her head, stops eating and takes the last crumbs from her bodice.* JEROME *bows his head and goes on chewing and putting food in his mouth.*

Lord god, lord god. The covetous man laugh in 'is secret yeart but thou art not mocked. Thou sent the whore t' the rich man's yate an' the poor man fell in her way but thou art not mocked.

WALLY. Amen.

JEROME. He yont finished yet, brother.

SON. Lord god, thou set thy cross for a sign-post afore the two ways. Lord god, shear the sheep in winter that he feel the blast. Amen.

WALLY *and* JOAN. Amen.

SHAKESPEARE *has stood up and walked slowly away. His movements and face express nothing.*

JEROME (*wiping his mouth with the back of his hand*). That'll do for grace. (*He stands.*) We'm off t' labour in the lord's vineyards.

SON. Yont do need t' laugh at good people, brother. You hev pains an' reasons for 'em I yont know, an' I hev mine. Only the sinner's branded front t' yead – an' that's sometime hid.

JEROME. Nothin' under my yat bar my yead.

JEROME *and* JOAN *go out. The* SON *stands in front of the gibbet.* WALLY *watches him.*

WALLY. What is it, brother?

SON. I'm larnin' t' face a sin so I know it in the street.

WALLY. Her's terrible changed.

SON. Death bring out her true life, brother. Look, her eyes be shut agin the truth. There's blood trickle down the corner a her mouth. Her teeth snap at her flesh while her die. Be solemn, brother, think a lord god. That's the face us turn to him even when us prays. Day an' day an' day he set the sun t'rise an' shine a way for his saints on earth an' us throw us shadow cross it. God weep.

WALLY. Halleluja! O rapture in the lord!

SON. Us sin an' go on all four in the grass. Us face is turned to dirt away from lord god.

WALLY. (*jumping*). Israel. Israel. Israel. Israel. Irsael. Israel. Israel.

WALLY. Praise an' glory. O tis terrible t' die so.

JUDITH (*off*). Father. Father.

SON ⎫ Worse, worse to live in sin. Lord god send death t' free
⎪ his sinner. Damnation's bliss when yo' know he chose
⎱ it for you.

WALLY ⎰ (*jumping*). Israel. Israel. Israel.

JUDITH *comes on right.*

JUDITH. My father.
SON. He were here. I sid a prayer but he turn away from the word.
WALLY. Spurned lord god like the roman in the judgement hall.
SON. Amen.
JUDITH (*calls*). Father.

JUDITH *stops in front of the* YOUNG WOMAN.

WALLY. She'll hev her full a fire now.
SON (*quietly. Watching* JUDITH). Harden your yeart for lord god,
sister. Dost matter t' him her beg when all eat out his yand?
No. Dost matter her burn the proud man's hall when he break
t' earth from toime t' toime? Dost matter her love a man when
he love all men –
JUDITH (*calls*). Father.
SON. Even the sinner's innocent. O harden your yeart with a glad-
some mind, good people. Tent for us t' question lord god's way.
Sin were 'er cross an her bore it afore us for a sign. Lord god
send the wolf an' the shepherd to the sheep.
WALLY. Amen.
SON. Amen.

The SON *and* WALLY *go out right.*

JUDITH (*calls*). Father.

SHAKESPEARE *comes on left.*

Are you blaming me? Is that what I've done now?
SHAKESPEARE. No. She'd have been caught. Burning . . .
JUDITH. Come home.
SHAKESPEARE. Later. (*He sits.*)

JUDITH. You're hungry.

SHAKESPEARE. Why do . . .? I thought I knew the questions. Have I forgotten them?

JUDITH. People will stroll out here to look after work. They'll talk if you sit there. We know what she was. (SHAKESPEARE *doesn't react.*) You were out all yesterday. Did you see her hang?

SHAKESPEARE. The baited bear. Tied to the stake. Its dirty coat needs brushing. Dried mud and spume. Pale dust. Big clumsy fists. Men bringing dogs through the gate. Leather collars with spikes. Loose them and fight. The bear wanders round the stake. It knows it can't get away. The chain. Dogs on three sides. Fur in the mouth. Deeper. (*The* OLD WOMAN *comes on upstage right.*) Flesh and blood. Strips of skin. Teeth scrapping bone. The bear will crush one of the skulls. Big feet slithering in dog's brain. Round the stake. On and on. The key in the warder's pocket. Howls. Roars. Men baiting their beast. On and on and on. And later the bear raises its great arm. The paw with a broken razor. And it looks as if it's making a gesture – it wasn't: only weariness or pain or the sun or brushing away the sweat – but it looks as if it's making a gesture to the crowd. Asking for one sign of grace, one no. And the crowd roars, for more blood, more pain, more beasts huddled together, tearing flesh and treading in living blood.

JUDITH. You don't like sport. Some bears dance.

SHAKESPEARE. In London they blinded a bear. Called Harry Hunks. The sport was to bait it with whips. Slash, slash. It couldn't see but it could hear. It grabbed the whips. Caught some of them. Broke them. Slashed back at the men. Slash, slash. The men stood round in a circle slashing at it. It was blind but they still chained it to the ground. Slash, slash. Then they sent an ape round on a horse. A thin hairy man or a child. You could see the pale skin under its arm when it jumped. Its teeth. The dogs tore it to pieces. The crowd howled. London. The queen cheered them on in shrill latin. The virgin often watched blood. Her father baited bears on the Thames. From boat to boat, slash, slash. They fell in and fought men in the water. He was the man in a mad house who says I'm king but he had a country to say it in.

JUDITH. I must go down. Someone must watch the house, count the glasses, knives, spoons. I shan't ask you to listen any more. You're only interested in your ideas. You treat us as enemies.

JUDITH walks upstage to the OLD WOMAN. The OLD WOMAN puts her arm round her and silently tries to comfort her.

SHAKESPEARE. What does it cost to stay alive? I'm stupefied at the suffering I've seen. The shapes huddled in misery that twitch away when you step over them. Women with shopping bags stepping over puddles of blood. What it costs to starve people. The chatter of those who hand over prisoners. The smile of men who see no further than the end of a knife. Stupefied. How can I go back to that? What can I do there? I talk to myself now. I know no one will ever listen.

The OLD WOMAN comes down to SHAKESPEARE.

OLD WOMAN. A gen'man's come from London. At the Golden Cross. (*She hands a note to SHAKESPEARE.*) He sent this up by me.

SHAKESPEARE. There's no higher wisdom of silence. No face brooding over the water. (*The OLD WOMAN glances helplessly up at JUDITH.*) No hand leading the waves to the shore as if it's saving a dog from the sea. When I go to my theatre I walk under sixteen severed heads on a gate. You hear bears in the pit while my characters talk.

OLD WOMAN. Now, sir. That's bin a longish winter. That's brought yo' down.

SHAKESPEARE. No other hand . . . no face . . . just these . . .

OLD WOMAN (*to JUDITH*). I'll bring him hwome.

JUDITH goes out.

SHAKESPEARE. Stupid woman! They stand under a gallows and ask if it rains. Terrible. Terrible. What is the right question? I said be still. I quietened the storms inside me. But the storm breaks outside. To have usurped the place of god, and lied . . .

OLD WOMAN. Why torment yo'self? You'm never harmed no –

SHAKESPEARE. And my daughter?

OLD WOMAN. No, no. Yo' yont named for cruelty. They say yo'm a generous man. Yo' looked arter me an' father. Give us one a your houses t' live in.

SHAKESPEARE (*points*). There's a coin. I saw it when I came up. Glittering in the grass.

OLD WOMAN (*goes immediately to where* SHAKESPEARE *pointed*). Here?

SHAKESPEARE. Perhaps the hangman dropped it.

OLD WOMAN (*picks up the coin*). We'm put a little by for later. Times change. Read your note.

SHAKESPEARE *is silent*. He doesn't move.

If yo' yont allow yo'self t' be helped, what shall us do? I'm afraid I'm like your daughter. I yont had no one t' talk to, no one t' share my loife. Juss father's prattle – an' he stay by me out a fear. Nothin' else. O a child love but he yont even a proper child. He yont more'n a wounded bud in a road. Tread on or go under a cart. I fed him. Kep him clane. Tak the washin' back when he steal it. Scare him so he yont hide t'much. I took a stick to him afore now, or he yont got no tay. But one day when he steal summat they'll be roight cross: shops're doin' bad or that's the weather. Then they'll hang him! His 'ole loife's a risk. I hope he die afore me. (*She shrugs*.) What'm I supposed a make a that? I yont afford arkst questions I yont know y'answers to. Well, you'm summat at peace now.

SHAKESPEARE. I went to the river yesterday. So quiet. They were all here. No fishing, no boats. One boy to mind the cattle – he was being punished. I watched the fish jump for flies. Then a swan flew by me up the river. On a straight line just over the water. A woman in a white dress running along an empty street. Its neck was rocking like a wave. I heard its breath when it flew by. Sighing. The white swan and the dark water. Straight down the middle of the river and round a curve out of sight. I could still hear its wings. God knows where it was going. So quiet and then silence. (*He gestures round.*) And here it was hot – (*He stands.*) – noise – dust . . . she saw none of this – (*He gestures to the horizon.*) the view . . . Where shall I go? London? Stay here? (*He goes to the gibbet. The* OLD WOMAN *watches him.*) Still perfect. Still beautiful.

In the far distance a bell peals briefly.

OLD WOMAN. No. Her's ugly. Her face is all a-twist. They put her legs in a sack count a she's dirty.

SHAKESPEARE. The marks on her face are men's hands. Won't they be washed away?

OLD WOMAN. She smell. She smell.

SHAKESPEARE *goes out. The* OLD WOMAN *goes to the place where she found the coin. She searches for a moment. She doesn't find anything. The bell stops. The* OLD WOMAN *looks across at the* YOUNG WOMAN. *Then she goes out.*

Part Two

FOUR

The Golden Cross. A large, irregular shaped room. Stone floor. Left, a few tables and benches, Right, a table and three chairs. A large open fire between them. Burning wood. Night. Lamps.

SHAKESPEARE *and* JONSON *are at the table right. Bottles and two glasses on the table. No one else in the room.*

SHAKESPEARE. How long did the theatre burn?

JONSON. Two hours.

SHAKESPEARE (*tapping the table*). When I was buying my house the owner was poisoned. By his son. A half-wit. They hanged him. Legal complications with the contract. My father was robbed by my mother's side of the family. That was property too.

JONSON. Coincidences.

SHAKESPEARE. But that such coincidences are possible . . . Jokes about my play setting the house on fire?

JONSON. What are you writing?

SHAKESPEARE. Nothing.

They drink.

JONSON. Not writing?

SHAKESPEARE. No.

JONSON. Why not?

SHAKESPEARE. Nothing to say.

JONSON. Doesn't stop others. Written out?

SHAKESPEARE. Yes.

They drink.

JONSON. Now, what are you writing?

SHAKESPEARE. Nothing.

JONSON. Down here for the peace and quiet? Find inspiration –
look for it, anyway. Work up something spiritual. Refined.
Can't get by with scrabbling it off in noisy corners any more.
New young men. Competition. Your recent stuff's been pretty
peculiar. What was The Winter's Tale about? I ask to be polite.

SHAKESPEARE. What are you writing?

JONSON. They say you've come down to study grammar. Or
history. Have you read my English Grammar? Let me sell you a
copy. I've got a few up in my room.

>   *Silence.* SHAKESPEARE *pours drinks.*

What am *I* writing? You've never shown any interest before.

SHAKESPEARE. Untrue.

JONSON. O, how many characters, enough big parts for the leads,
a bit of comedy to bring them in – usual theatre-owner's questions. Trying to pick my brains now? Run out of ideas?

>   *They drink.*

Nice to see you again. I'm off to Scotland soon. Walking. Alone.
Well, no one would come with me. Might be a book in it. Eat out
on London gossip. The Scots are very credulous – common
sense people are always superstitious, aren't they. Can't
imagine you walking to Scotland. That sort of research is too
real!

SHAKESPEARE (*smiles. Starts to stand*). Well.

JONSON. Don't go. Sit down. Would you like to read my new
play? It's up in my room. Won't take a minute.

SHAKESPEARE. No.

JONSON. Nice to see you again. Honest William.

SHAKESPEARE. I wouldn't read it. It would lie there.

JONSON. What is it? Tired? Not well? (SHAKESPEARE *starts to
stand.*) Sit down. (*He pours drinks.*) Wife better?

SHAKESPEARE. No.

JONSON. Wrong subject. D'you like the quiet?

SHAKESPEARE. What quiet?

> *They drink.*

JONSON. What are you writing? (*Slight pause.*) The theatre told
me to ask.
SHAKESPEARE (*shakes his head*). Sorry.
JONSON. What d'you do?
SHAKESPEARE. There's the house. People I'm responsible for.
The garden's too big. Time goes. I'm surprised how old I've
got.
JONSON. You always kept yourself to yourself. Well, you certainly
didn't like me. Or what I wrote. Sit down. I hate writing. Fat
white fingers excreting dirty black ink. Smudges. Shadows.
Shit. Silence.
SHAKESPEARE. You're a very good writer.
JONSON. Patronizing bastard.

> *Slight pause. They drink.*

You don't want to quarrel with me. I killed one once. Fellow
writer. Only way to end a literary quarrel. Put my sword in him.
Like a new pen. The blood flowed as if inspired. Then the Old
Bailey. I was going to hang. That's carrying research too far. I
could read so they let me off. Proper respect for learning.
Branded my thumb. A child's alphabet: T for Tyburn. I've
been in prison four times. Dark smelly places. No gardens.
Sorry yours is too big. They kept coming in and taking people
out to cut bits off them. Their hands. Take off their noses.
Cut their stomachs open. Rummage round inside with a dirty
fist and drag everything out. The law. Little men going out
through the door. White. Shaking. Even staggering. I ask, is it
necessary? What's your life been like? Any real blood, any
prison? Four times? Don't go, don't go. I want to touch you
for a loan. I know I'm not human. My father died before I was
born. That desperate to avoid me. My eyes are too close together. Look. A well known fact. I used to have so much good

will when I was young. That's what's necessary, isn't it? Good
will. In the end. O god.

Silence. They drink.

Yes.

Silence.

What are you writing?

SHAKESPEARE. I think you're a very good writer. I made them
put on your first play.

JONSON. God, am I that bad? In prison they threatened to cut
off my nose. And ears. They didn't offer to work on my eyes.
Life doesn't seem to touch you, I mean soil you. You walk by
on the clean pavement. I climb tall towers to show I'm clever.
Others do tricks in the gutter. You are serene. Serene. I'm
going to make you drunk and watch you spew. You aren't well,
I can see that! Something's happening to your will. You're
being sapped. I think you're dying. What a laugh! Are you
getting hollow? Why don't you get up? Walk out? Why are you
listening to my hysterical crap? Don't worry about me. I'll
survive. I've lived through two religious conversions. I thrive
on tearing myself to bits. I even bought enough poison. Once.
In a moment of strength. (*He takes a small bottle from his collar.
It hangs round his neck on a chain.*) I was too weak to take it.
Hung the cross here in my catholic period. (*He takes the top off
the bottle.*) Look: coated in sugar. Like to lick my poison? I
licked one once to try. (SHAKESPEARE *doesn't react.*) Well, it's
not the best. All I could afford. Little corner shop in London.

SHAKESPEARE. Give it to me.

JONSON. Sentimental whiner. You wouldn't uncross your legs if I
ate the lot. You're upset I might give it to someone else. (*He
puts the bottle back in his collar.*) I should live in the country.
No – I'd hear myself talk. When I went sight seeing in the mad
house there was a young man who spent all his time stamping on
his shadow. Punched it. Went for it with a knife. Tried to cut

the head off. Anything to be free. The knife on the stone. The noise. Sparks.

They drink.

I helped to uncover the gunpowder plot. Keep in with the top.

They drink.

Your health. I'm always saying nice things about you, Serenity. Of course, I touch on your lack of education, or as I put it genuine ignorance. But you can't ignore an elephant when it waves at you with its trunk, can you. You taking this down? Base something on me. A minor character who comes on for five minutes while the lead's off changing his clothes or making a last effort to learn his lines? Shall I tell you something about me? I hate. Yes – isn't that interesting! I keep it well hidden but it's true: I hate. A short hard word. Begins with a hiss and ends with a spit: hate. To say it you open your mouth as if you're bringing up: hate. I hate you, for example. For preference actually. Hate's far more jealous than love. You can't satisfy it by the gut or the groin. A terrible appetite. Interrupt me. Speak. Sob. Nothing? I'm not afraid to let myself be insulted.

The SON, WALLY, JEROME *and* JOAN *come in right.*

SON (*pointing left*). Over there.

The SON *goes out right again. The others sit.*

WALLY. They'm followed us.
JEROME. No matter. They'll know who t'was.
WALLY. They'm followed us. I were neigh on slaughtered. One a Combe's men heaved a rock at us when I were scramblin' out the ditch. I'm certain-sure they'm followed us. Where's us shovels?
JEROME. I hid they in the hedge out back.
JOAN (*looking across at* SHAKESPEARE *and* JONSON). Careful, there's gen'men here.

JEROME. Too drunk t' hear if yo' shouted.

WALLY. Git the mud off yo'. That show what us bin up to. Us don't ought-a done it. That'll only start more row.

JEROME. That's us land. Shall us sit down an' let 'em rob it? How I live then? How I feed my wife an' little-uns?

JOAN. Hush.

JEROME. I'll break Combe's neck.

JONSON. Where was I? Yes: hate. I hate you because you smile. Right up to *under* your eyes. Which are set the right distance apart. O I've wiped the smile off now. I hate your health. I'm sure you'll die in a healthy way. Well at least you're dying. That's incense to scatter on these burning coals. I hate your long country limbs. I've seen you walking along the city streets like a man going over his own fields. So simple. A simple stride. So beautiful and simple. You see why I hate you. How have they made you so simple? Tell me, Will? Please. How have they made you so good? You even know when it's time to die. Come down here to die quietly in your garden or an upstairs room. My death will be terrible. I'll linger on in people's way, poor, thick, dirty, empty, a mess. I go on and on, why can't I stop? I even talk shit now. To know the seasons of life and death and walk quietly on the path between them. Hate is like a clown armed with a knife. He must draw blood to cap the joke, you know? Well, have you got a new play, it has to be a comedy, rebuilding is expensive, they'd like you to invest. Think about it. You may come up with an idea, or manage to steal one. But it must be in time for next season.

Silence.

My life's been one long self-insult. It came on with puberty.

Silence. JONSON *drinks.*

Teach me something.

SHAKESPEARE *falls across the table and spills his glass.*

God.

> JONSON *tries to dry* SHAKESPEARE *with a napkin. He sets him up in his chair.* SHAKESPEARE *slumps forward again. The* SON *comes on with a bottle and glasses.* JOAN *pours.*

SON. They yont give up.

JOAN. No more'll us. (*She hands him a drink. He waves it aside.*)

SON (*rocking slightly*). Rich thieves plunderin' the earth. Think on the poor trees an' grass an' beasts, all neglect an' stood in the absence a god. One year no harvest'll come, no seed'll grow in the plants, no green, no cattle yont leave their stall, stand hud-dled-to in the hovel, no hand'll turn water in their trough, the earth'll die an' be covered with scars: the mark a dust where a beast rot in the sand. Where there's no lord god there's a wilderness.

WALLY. Don't go forth in it now, brother. (*To the others.*) He's allus close t' tears. (*To the* SON.) Don't git took up.

JOAN (*offers the* SON *the drink again*). Yo' hev this. That's cold out there t'night. (*The* SON *doesn't take it.*)

WALLY. The waters a Babylon run by his door.

SON (*rocking slightly*). The absence a god, the wilderness . . . neglect . . .

> COMBE *comes in. He goes to the* SON.

COMBE. You've been here all evening.

SON (*nods*). Even', Mr Combe.

COMBE (*to* JONSON). How long have they been here?

JONSON. When I drink my eyes swim closer together. One, two, nine, ten peasants . . .

> SHAKESPEARE *is still slumped forward on the table.*

COMBE (*to the* SON). I thought the brothers didn't swill.

SON. We may quench thirst in an orderly 'ouse.

COMBE. After labour.

JONSON *gets up and goes out right. As he goes he talks. The*
others ignore him. He is drunk but controlled.

COMBE. Every time you fill my ditches I'll dig them out. Every time you pull down my fence I'll put it back. There'll be more broken fences.

JONSON. To spend my life wandering through quiet fields. Charm fish from the water with a song. Gather simple eggs. Muse with my reflection in quiet water having the accents of philosophy. And lie at last in some cool mossy grave where maidens come to make vows over my corpse. (*He goes.*)

SON (*to* WALLY). Note that.

COMBE. Be very careful on Sunday. Wear the right cap and go to the parish church – not some holy hovel out in the fields. Keep to the law. Don't come up in front of me on the bench.

SON. Whose interest's that protectin'? Public or yourn?

COMBE. You trespass on my land. Fight my men. Trample my crop. Now you turn me into the devil. The town will benefit from what I'm doing. So will the poor.

JEROME (*quietly*). S'long's they'm still alive.

COMBE. What? (JEROME *doesn't answer.* COMBE *turns to the* SON.) There's a division in this country. We're not just fighting for land. Listen. I've seen suffering, I've caused some of it – and I try to stop it. But I know this: there'll always be real suffering, real stupidity and greed and violence. And there can be no civilization till you've learned to live with it. I live in the real world and try to make it work. There's nothing more moral than that. But you live in a world of dreams! Well, what happens when you have to wake up? You find that real people can't live in your dreams. They don't fit, they're not good or sane or noble enough. So you turn to common violence and begin to destroy them. (*He stops.*) Why should I talk to you? You can't listen. (*To* JEROME.) You hold your farm on a lease. When you die your son has to pay a fee before he inherits it. That fee isn't fixed – it's decided by the landlord, my brother-in-law. We work with anyone who shows good will. But there can only be one master.

JONSON *comes back. He carries a bottle.*

SON. A sexton's diggin' your ditches, Combe.

WALLY. Amen.

SON. An' yo'll be buried in 'em.

JOAN. So dig 'em deep. Israel.

WALLY. Israel. Israel. Israel.

JONSON. Where can you buy a good spade? I'm sure there's a book in it. Should find a sale. Sound practical manual in a good, simple, craftsman's style.

COMBE. Grown men acting like children.

COMBE *goes out.*

SON. God take us on a long journey. That man's prophetical. We see the same truth from odd sides but us both know tis the truth.

WALLY (*softly*). Glory. Glory.

SON. I looked cross a great plain into his eyes. A sword were put into my yand. The lord god a peace arm us. We must go back an' fill up they ditches agin t'night.

JEROME. T'night?

SON. Whenever he turn his back. Every toime.

JEROME. Us'll come.

JOAN. No.

JEROME. Ah! There's only one master. When yo' put your yand in your pocket now yo' find another yand there.

The SON *and* WALLY *go towards the door.*

JONSON. Shepherds –

The SON *and* WALLY *ignore him and go out.*

JONSON (*to* JOAN *and* JEROME). – fill your bowls.

JOAN (*to* JEROME). That's a full bottle. Wasted on them in that state.

JEROME. While us wait.

> JOAN *and* JEROME *go to* JONSON's *table.* SHAKESPEARE *is still slumped forward.* JEROME *recognizes him.*

JONSON (*shaking* SHAKESPEARE). The pilgrims have come.

JEROME. We yont better sit with the gen'man.

SHAKESPEARE. Sit down.

> JONSON *starts to fill their glasses.*

JONSON. Was that man your enemy? Call him back and let me kill him for you.

SHAKESPEARE. You've been filling the ditches.

JEROME. No.

SHAKESPEARE. Lie to me. Lie. Lie. You have to lie to me now.

> WALLY *runs in. He has a shovel.*

WALLY. Snow! Snow!

JOAN. Snow!

WALLY. Late snow! A portent! A sign!

JEROME (*seeing the shovel*). Git that shovel out!

JOAN. Snow! Shall us still go?

JEROME (*pushing* WALLY). Git that out! Yo' fool!

WALLY. What? Snow! Snow!

SHAKESPEARE. Lie to me. Lie to me.

> WALLY *and* JEROME *go out.* JOAN *follows them.*

JONSON. They went? Was it my talk? I talk too much. (*He sits. They drink.*) I hope you're paying. I certainly can't afford to drink like this. You said something about a loan. (SHAKESPEARE *puts money on the table.*) I thought it was just the drink talking. (*He counts the money.*) In paradise there'll be a cash tree, and the sages will sit under it. You can't manage anything better?

You wouldn't notice it. I had to borrow to bury my little boy. I still owe on the grave. (*He puts the money in his pocket.*) I suppose you buried your boy in best oak. Sit down, sit down.

FIVE

Open space. Flat, white, crisp, empty. The fields, paths, roads, bushes and trees are covered with smooth clean snow. It has stopped snowing. Shakespeare comes on drunk. JONSON's *poison bottle hangs from a chain in his hand.*

SHAKESPEARE. My house. There at the bottom of the fields. No, I won't go in. How dark it is. No lamps. The door is a hole. The windows are ditches with water in. (*He pauses. Looks round.*) How clean and empty the snow is. A sea without life. An empty glass. Still smooth. No footprints. No ruts. No marks of weapons or hoes dragged through the ground. Only my foot-prints behind me – and they're white . . . white . . . (*He looks towards the house again.*) How long did I live there? So dark. No footprints up to the door. No one's gone down the path brushing against the hedge. The snow's still on top. In the morning there'll be dead birds under the hedge. Their winter colours will be bright in the snow. Their wings folded in for warmth, not stretched out to fly between the snow and the moon . . . The water and the earth are frozen together . . . One piece of ice . . .

A snowball hits him. The OLD MAN *comes on. He is excited, running in the cold has made his voice high.*

OLD MAN. A hit. A hit.

SHAKESPEARE. Where have you been?

OLD MAN. A hit. I bin aimin' snowballs at a snowman. (*He throws a snowball at* SHAKESPEARE.) A hit. A hit. (*He dances.*) Look at that snow, boy. I heard yo' talkin' things t' yo'self.

SHAKESPEARE. Are you cold?

OLD MAN. No. I play. I flap my arms an' run up an' down. Come t' see my snowman.

SHAKESPEARE. Too far.

OLD MAN (*Throws a snowball at* SHAKESPEARE). A hit. Ten, nothin'. Try t' hit us, boy. (*He puts a snowball in* SHAKESPEARE's *hand.*) Try. Try. Please.

SHAKESPEARE *throws the snowball at him.*

SHAKESPEARE. It hit.

OLD MAN (*laughing derisively*). The legs, the legs, the legs yont count. Still fourteen, nothin'. Throw for the neck.

SHAKESPEARE. Were you on the hill?

OLD MAN. Ah. For a last see. A last toime. Then I saw summat come cross t' fields. A great white thing. That were a cloud I thought! Low. Then that turn t' snow. O pretty! That did fall fast. I saw the fields turn white. (*He laughs.*) She had a little heap set top on her yead. Like a cap. I made a slide down side t' hill. Whee! I hed such a toime. I like snow. Yont yo'? Then they rabbits all come t' see. You charm a rabbit by your play. They set theyselfs round in a circle. Heads on one side. I grabs one an' broke his neck for'n. (*He holds out a dead rabbit.*) Bad. Some'un elsen. Mustn't take. (*He grins.*) But my wife yont row me out when I come hwome. She'll hide it in the pot smart. (*He pats his pockets.*) I got onions here. Carrot here. Egg. Us'll hev a feast. Early greens.

Four of five dark FIGURES *pass quickly over the top of the stage. They are huddled and quiet. One stops and points at* SHAKESPEARE *and the* OLD MAN.

FIGURE I (*low*). 'Oo's that?

FIGURE II (*stops, low*). Drunks.

All the FIGURES *go out right.*

SHAKESPEARE. A light's on in my house. They're trying to get in
   my room.

OLD MAN. They'll be out arter yo' now. I flare up do my wife
   come after me. She know the shape a my fist. Now her wait up
   till I'm in an' lock up arter us. I yont see no sight a my snowman
   in this snow.

The OLD MAN *wanders out.*

SHAKESPEARE. The door's opened. I drank too much. I must be
   calm. Don't fall about in front of them. Why did I drink all
   that? Fool! Fool! At my age . . . Why not? I am a fool. Why did
   I come back here. I wanted to meet some god by the river. Ask
   him questions. See his mouth open and the lips move. Hear
   simple things that move mountains and stop the blood before it
   hits the earth. Stop it so there's time to think. I was wrong to
   come – mistakes, mistakes. But I can't go back. That hate,
   anger –

JUDITH *comes in. She wears a green cloak.*

JUDITH. Walk all night in the fields if you like. I don't mind. But
   not when it's snowed. Mother's crying.

SHAKESPEARE. Who woke her?

JUDITH. It's late and I'm tired.

SHAKESPEARE. Who?

JUDITH. Another scene.

SHAKESPEARE. Why did you do it? What can she do? Cry!

JUDITH. When you behave like a child you'll be treated like one.

SHAKESPEARE. Listen. You'll get my property between you when
   I'm dead. When I ran away from your mother and went to
   London – I was so bored, she's such a silly woman, obstinate,
   and you take after her. Forgive me, I know that's cruel, sordid,

but it's such an effort to be polite any more. That other age when I ran away, I couldn't cut you out, you were my flesh, but I thought I could make you forgive me: I started to collect for you. I loved you with money. The only thing I can afford to give you now is money. But money always turns to hate. If I tried to be nice to you now it would be sentimental. You'd have to understand why I hate you, respect me for it, even love me for it. How can you? I treated you so badly. I made you vulgar and ugly and cheap. I corrupted you.

JUDITH. Go on. I'm not listening. I'm young and this coat's warm. I'll wait till you drop and then have you dragged in.

SHAKESPEARE. Don't be angry because I hate you, Judith. My hatred isn't angry. It's cold and formal. I wouldn't harm you. I'll help you, give my life for you – all in hatred. There's no limit to my hate. It can't be satisfied by cruelty. It's destroyed too much to be satisfied so easily. Only truth can satisfy it now. I don't think all this matters to you, I can't hate you more than when I say that.

JUDITH *goes out.*

The last snow this year. Perhaps the last snow I shall see. The last fall. (*He kneels on the ground and picks up some snow.*) How cold. (*He half smiles.*) How perfect, but it only lasts one night. When I was young I'd have written on it with a stick. A song. The moon over the snow, a woman stares at her dead . . . What? In the morning the sun would melt it into mortality. Writing in the snow – a child's hand fumbling in an old man's beard, and in the morning the old man dies, goes, taking the curls from the child's fingers into the grave, and the child laughs and plays under the dead man's window. New games. Now *I'm* old. Where is the child to touch me and lead me to the grave? Serene. Serene. Is that how they see me? (*He laughs a little.*) I didn't know.

The dark FIGURES *run back across the top of the stage. Their heavy breathing is heard. They go off left.*

Snow. It doesn't melt. My hand's cold. (*He breathes on the snow in his hand.*) It doesn't melt. I must be very cold. Serene. How? When you're running from hangers and breakers and killers. The mad clown still nurses the child.

Far upstage a shot and a spurt of flame.

Every writer writes in other men's blood. The trivial, and the real. There's nothing else to write in. But only a god or a devil can write in other men's blood and not ask why they spilt it and what it cost. Not this hand, that's always melted snow . . .

SHAKESPEARE *lies forward on the ground. A dark* FIGURE *appears upstage. It cries and whimpers weakly and then vanishes.*

I didn't want to die. I could lie in this snow a whole life. I can think now, the thoughts come so easily over the snow and under my shroud. New worlds. Keys turning new locks – pushing the iron open like lion's teeth. Wolves will drag me through the snow. I'll sit in their lair and smile and be rich. In the morning or when I die the sun will rise and melt it all away. The dream. The wolves. The iron teeth. The snow. The wind. My voice. A dream that leads to sleep. (*He sits up.*) I'm dead now. Soon I shall fall down. If I wasn't dead I could kill myself. What is the ice inside me? The plague is hot – this is so cold. The truth means nothing when you hate. Was anything done? Was anything done? I sit in a wound as large as a valley. The sides are smooth and cold and grey. I sit at the bottom and cry at my own death.

The OLD WOMAN *comes in.*

OLD WOMAN. Your daughter come a-knock-knock at my door. Darlint, I say, yont no call t' fret, I'm set up waitin'. Fetch him in, she say. That's twice t'day, I say. Last toime yo' was an okkard fuss. Father's out too.

The OLD WOMAN *helps* SHAKESPEARE *to his feet.*

'Ow yo' people carry on. (*She feels him.*) Good lor, you're froze.

SHAKESPEARE. Silly. Staying out here. What have I done?

OLD WOMAN. Yo' had your reasons.

SHAKESPEARE. Drunk.

OLD WOMAN. Hev yo' yeard summat a while back? I yeard a noise, blowed if I yont. I yeard thunder in snow one toime. Toime I were a gal. They say I were a dazzler. That seem afore your father step into the world! – but I remember on it. I thought I saw summat run long the lane a while back. These eyes . . . I wish father yont stop out when that's jippy. Yont make no wish yo' can't grant yo'sel.

SHAKESPEARE. Take me in, take me in.

OLD WOMAN. Yes, sir, I'm sorry.

SHAKESPEARE. Light a fire in my room. I'm cold.

OLD WOMAN. O'course. Yes, yes.

The OLD WOMAN *helps* SHAKESPEARE *out.*

SIX

Bedroom. Left, a bed with a needlework cover. Close to it a bedstand. A wooden chair. Right, a door. SHAKESPEARE *lies in bed. The* OLD WOMAN *stands in the room.*

OLD WOMAN. I ought-a go down. (SHAKESPEARE *doesn't answer.*) I'll stay a while longer. My son'll say when that's toime.

(*Silence. She sits on the chair.*) Shall us set down? I'm that tired.
(*She spreads her fingers and looks at her hands.*) I wanted him t'
die first. Seem wrong now. He were lyin' in that snow an' I walk
by him. Hed he say where he'd bin? (*No answer.*) Nicet if he
sid summat a show he know he'd bin looked arter . . . Could yo'
eat summat? Shall us let yo' sleep?

SHAKESPEARE. Was anything done?

OLD WOMAN. Yo' ought-a sleep. Why yont yo' try? . . . That all
come out a closin they fields. I told yo' long ago in the garden:
that'll cause trouble. Yo' yont listen. Sign a piece of piper an'
that's all yo' thought on. Call that 'elp? Our house's quiet now
he's gone. No one come or go, do they knock first an' ask if
I'm in. A stranger's house. All they years.

SHAKESPEARE. Was anything done?

OLD WOMAN. Your daft questions. I yont harm no one's far's I
could stop it. I look arter the two on us well's I might. (*Slight
pause.*) He'd bin t' see that dead woman, that's 'ow it ended.
(*She shrugs.*) He warnt greedy for money loike some men. I
yont know . . .

SHAKESPEARE. It's so cold.

OLD WOMAN. That yont his woman neither. That warnt n'more'n
his game. 'I want t' go out t' play. I'm tired a playin' indoor.'
He wanted summat a child want. I yont know what. (*She
shrugs.*) Well, yo' break a cup yo' put it t'gither. Yont kip
arksin' 'oo brok it. That's all as is.

JUDITH (*off*). Father.

SHAKESPEARE *motions the* OLD WOMAN *to be quiet.*

JUDITH (*off*). Mother's here to see you.

SHAKESPEARE (*quietly to the* OLD WOMAN). I'm asleep.

JUDITH (*off*). Father.

Silence.

SHAKESPEARE (*quietly to the* OLD WOMAN). Has she gone?

OLD WOMAN (*goes to the door and calls softly*). Judy, dear?

No answer. SHAKESPEARE *gets out of bed, goes to the door and listens.*

SHAKESPEARE (*quietly to the* OLD WOMAN). She's there.

The OLD WOMAN *goes to the chair and sits down again.*

OLD WOMAN. They'll level with me for this.

SHAKESPEARE *walks away from the door. Silence. There is a knock on it.*

JUDITH (*off*). Father, mother's here. (*Knock.*) Father. (*Knock.*) Open this door.

Outside an OLD WOMAN *begins to cry. More knocking on the door. The door handle is rattled. The knocking gets louder.*

JUDITH (*off*). Father, unlock this door. Mother's crying. Father, I know you can hear.

Outside the two women bang on the door. The crying is louder and wilder. Suddenly it becomes hysterical. The OLD WOMAN *gets up and slowly and methodically makes the bed.*

JUDITH (*off*). Father. Let us in. How dare you. You treat us like animals. Father. Why don't you come and hit her. You're cruel enough. You've done it before. Open the door and kick her. Father. We hate you. You're cruel. Wicked. Ugly. You beast.

The door is violently banged, kicked and shaken. Someone scratches it. Outside the OLD WOMAN *gasps and shrieks hysterically.*

JUDITH (*off*). Mother, get up. She's fallen down. Don't cover your ears – I'll make you hear. Make you. Make you. Make you. She's on the ground tearing her clothes. Look, her hands are bleeding.

SHAKESPEARE (*almost to himself*). It's so cold now.

JUDITH (*off*). Mother dear! Stop it! No. Don't. Help. Father.

SHAKESPEARE (*as before*). Cold. Cold.

OLD WOMAN (*quietly*). I'll open the door.

SHAKESPEARE. No. It's put on. Thirty-five years. All like this. (*He points to the bedside stand.*) My will. There. Fetch it.

JUDITH (*off*). You'll be punished. There's a god in heaven. She's tearing her hair. Terrible. Terrible. All my life. This. Time after time. I'll kill myself.

The OLD WOMAN *rummages through papers on the bedside stand. She finds three sheets lying together.*

SHAKESPEARE. Those. Yes, yes, those.

The OLD WOMAN *brings the sheets to* SHAKESPEARE. *They both stand by the door.*

JUDITH (*off*). She's clutching her heart. What is it?

Outside the OLD WOMAN *gasps stertorously.*

SHAKESPEARE (*quietly, with amused contempt*). Clutching! (*He pushes the sheets under the door.*) It's all there. Your legal share. And the bed.

The sheets are snatched through from the other side. The crying becomes lower but goes on.

JUDITH (*off*). Stand up. I'll help you. Try. (*The voices start to move away from the door.*) He won't let us in. I told you not to come down. I won't let you any more. We'll never speak to him again. He'll learn when it's too late. There.

The crying dies away. It is quiet.

OLD WOMAN. Is that what her come for?

SHAKESPEARE. No. She'll be quieter now.

OLD WOMAN. Bed's made.

SHAKESPEARE. The chair. (*He sits in the chair. He closes his eyes. He is weak and tired.*) Cold. There's a draft. That door. Did they break it? (*The* OLD WOMAN *glances at the door.*) I

must be quiet. White worms excreting black ink. Scratch.
Scratch.

OLD WOMAN. What?

SHAKESPEARE. Was anything done? Was anything done?

A knock on the door.

OLD WOMAN. Yes?

SON (*off*). Mother.

The OLD WOMAN *opens the door. The* SON *comes in.*

'Oo's bin a-scratchin' your door? Half the paint's took off.

OLD WOMAN. Are they ready?

SON. Ah.

OLD WOMAN. I'll git into my coat. (*She pauses.*) I'll arkst summat
first. Hev yo' took a gun with yo'?

SON. Us yont shot him. Us warn't armed.

OLD WOMAN. Then I'll walk t' church with yo'. (*To* SHAKE-
SPEARE.) Goodbye.

SON. I'll follow directly.

The OLD WOMAN *goes out. The* SON *locks the door behind her.*

What hev yo' see?

SHAKESPEARE. Nothing.

SON. Yo' must hev. That were snow an' moon. Like day.

SHAKESPEARE. I wouldn't choose to lie while I'm dying. (*The*
SON *watches* SHAKESPEARE *for a moment.* SHAKESPEARE
closes his eyes again.) You can tell. Can't you. My face.

SON. Yo're very poorly.

SHAKESPEARE. I spent so much of my youth, my best energy
. . . for this: New Place. Somewhere to be sane in. It was all a
mistake. There's a taste of bitterness in my mouth. My
stomach pumps it up when I think of myself . . . I could have
done so much. (*The* SON *goes to the door and listens for a sound
outside.*) Absurd! Absurd! I howled when they suffered, but

they were whipped and hanged so that I could be free. That is
the right question: not why did I sign one piece of paper? – no,
no, even when I sat at my table, when I put on my clothes, I
was a hangman's assistant, a gaoler's errand boy. If children go
in rags we make the wind. If the table's empty we blight
the harvest. If the roof leaks we send the storm. God made the
elements but we inflict them on each other. Everything can be
stolen, property and qualities of the mind. But stolen things
have no value. Pride and arrogance are the same when they're
stolen. Even serenity.

    The SON *has come to* SHAKESPEARE.

SON. Everyone looked the same in the moonlight. I shot him.
SHAKESPEARE. So you met. The son and the father.
SON (*quietly*). I yont give meself up. Us'll foight for us land. Out-
    side a me they'd give in. I'll go off later. When mother's settled.
    T'ent easy t'be with her now. T'ent decent.
SHAKESPEARE. A murderer telling a dead man the truth. Are we
    the only people who can afford the truth?

    A knock at the door.

SON (*calls*). What?
COMBE (*off*). Combe here.
SHAKESPEARE. Unlock it.

    The SON *unlocks the door.* COMBE *comes in. The* SON *locks*
    the door behind him. COMBE *stares at the* SON *and then turns*
    to SHAKESPEARE.

COMBE. Not disturbing you, I hope? Everything all right?
SHAKESPEARE. Some tablets. There. On the table. Please.

    COMBE *goes to the bedside stand and picks up* JONSON's
    poison bottle.

COMBE. These?
SHAKESPEARE. Thank you.

COMBE (*gives the bottle to* SHAKESPEARE. *To the* SON). I'm
   sorry about your father. Decent man. This won't stop the
   enclosure.

SON. Your side shot him.

COMBE. I told my men no guns, only sticks. One of them may
   have disobeyed me – out of fear of you. Perhaps it was your own
   people. (*To* SHAKESPEARE.) I came to ask if you saw or heard
   anything. I'm told you were there.

SHAKESPEARE. Nothing.

COMBE. Pity. It's the magistrate's duty to ask.

   THE SON *laughs.*

If it's one of my men he'll be punished.

   SHAKESPEARE *starts to take the tablets.*

SON. What difference is that to us? Yo' take us land an' if us foight
   for'n – we'm criminals.

COMBE. You've a right to justice on your father's behalf. It's my
   duty to give it to you. Even though you're morally responsible
   for his death.

SON. Morally responsible! (*He laughs.*) He yont see! He yont see!
   He talk 'bout his law loike that had summat a do with justice!
   How can yo' give us justice, boy? Yo'm a thief. When yo' hang
   the man that kill my father, what yo' doin'? Is that justice? No –
   yo'm protectin' your thievin'.

COMBE (*to* SHAKESPEARE). I hope you're on your feet soon.

   The SON *unlocks the door for* COMBE. COMBE *goes out.*
   The SON *locks the door again.* SHAKESPEARE *takes more*
   tablets.

SON. I'll go away – where there's still space. I want t'be free. I cry
   for that. Sometoime when I'm out in the fields I climb a tall
   tree an' set stride the top an' cry. Let me be free. Liberty. Where
   no one stand 'tween me an' my god, no one listen when I raise

the song a praise, an' I walk by god's side with curtesy an' fear nothin', as candid loike a child. (SHAKESPEARE *takes more tablets.*) So us'll go away. Us plans is laid. Us'll take nowt bar bible an' plough. (*Pause. His voice changes.*) I yont had no proper toime t'reflect orderly on my father's dyin' – what with the land an' arrangements an' that. I kill him. That'll have t' be go over proper in my yead. Lord god'll say. Likely he done it a purpose. Why else'd he afflict one a his chosen with a harsh cross? The yand a god's in it someplace. (*He goes to the door and unlocks it.*) The kẹy?

SHAKESPEARE. Go and bury your father.

> *The* SON *opens the door. He stops in the doorway.* SHAKE-SPEARE *takes more tablets.*

SON (*quietly*). . . . When yo' think on't, t'ent so sure I shot him neither. I fire a gun – I yont hide no truth. That yont mean I shot him. Someone else'n moight a fired. Death on an un-armed man – that's more loike the sort a think Combe'd get up to. That want sortin' out in my yead. I may have done meself a wrong.

> *The* SON *goes out. He leaves the door open.*

SHAKESPEARE. How long have I been dead? When will I fall down? Looking for rings on beggars' fingers. Mistakes . . . mistakes . . . Was anything done? (*He takes another tablet.*) Years waiting . . . fed . . . washing the dead . . . Was anything done? . . . Was anything done? (*He looks at a tablet in his hand.*) Dead sugar. (*He swallows it.*) Was anything done?

> *He falls from the chair onto the floor.* JUDITH *comes into the room. She sees* SHAKESPEARE. *She controls her panic. The funeral bell begins to toll. It is close, but not so loud as in the garden.* JUDITH *goes to* SHAKESPEARE *and quickly makes him comfortable on the floor. He twitches and jerks.*

JUDITH. Nothing. A little attack.

> *She hurries to the bedside stand. She searches through it agitatedly. She throws papers aside. She tears some.* SHAKESPEARE *whimpers and shivers.*

JUDITH (*to herself as she searches*). Nothing. Nothing.

> JUDITH *runs to the door and shouts up.*

Nothing. If he made a new will his lawyer's got it.

> JUDITH *runs back to the bed. She is crying. She searches under the pillows.* SHAKESPEARE *has killed himself.*

JUDITH (*crying*). Nothing.

> JUDITH *searches under the sheets. She kneels down and searches under the bed. She cries. She stands and searches under the mattress.*

PASSION

A play for CND

Passion was first presented in an open-air production at Alexandra Park Racecourse by the Royal Court Theatre as part of the CND Festival of Life on Easter Sunday, 11 April 1971 with the following cast:

NARRATOR	Chris Malcolm
OLD WOMAN	Susan Engel
DEAD SOLDIER	Marc McManus
QUEEN	Penelope Wilton
PRIME MINISTER	Nigel Hawthorne
MAGICIAN	Roddy Maude-Roxby
CHRIST	Norman Beaton
BUDDHA	Bob Hoskins

Directed by Bill Bryden
Designed by Di Seymour
Staged Managed by Peter Allday
Amplification organized by Dick Lock

These scenes can be played indoors or outdoors. Microphones can be used. The Narrator need not be seen. The characters should be played as types or even archetypes, not individuals. Clothes and make-up should be exaggerated. The title of each section should be given by the Narrator, or shown, before it is played.

THE GARDEN

NARRATOR. There was once an old woman. Her only son was made a soldier and sent to war. When he was killed his body was sent back to her. She was sitting in her garden when it was carried in on a stretcher.

The OLD WOMAN *sits daydreaming on a stool. The* DEAD SOLDIER *is carried in on a stretcher. It is covered with a blanket. The* OLD WOMAN *rises and goes to the stretcher. She makes the gestures and movements of mourning while the voice of the* DEAD SOLDIER *speaks for her.*

DEAD SOLDIER. They have killed my son. They took my only child away and dressed him up for a holiday. They put money in his pocket and he got drunk. He sailed away in a boat to see the world. They said people will welcome you everywhere and you will be called their friend. They said you will destroy the people's foes and punish the wicked. Then they had a battle and the two armies destroyed each other. Afterwards the soldier was lost. He wandered about for days in a cold and empty wilderness. He was afraid to sleep because marauders were cutting the wounded men's throats and robbing them. All he'd had to eat for a week was the biscuits and bits of bread he found in the pockets of the dead soldiers' uniforms. One morning he was lying in a ditch half mad. He heard the wind blowing and he thought it was calling his name. He lifted his head and was shot in the face. He was a young, healthy, strong soldier and it was very difficult for him to die. When it was getting dark the crows found him and he felt their claws as they landed on his face and he heard them cawing. Then he felt them picking at strips of his flesh as if they were tugging worms from the earth, and in a little while he died.

NARRATOR. The old woman stopped crying.

OLD WOMAN. Well, I must stop crying and think about money. After all, I have to live. It's very difficult for an old woman on her own. I can't manage and that's a fact. I need my son to keep me. I shall go to the queen and ask for him back. She's clever and lots of clever men and magicians work for her – she can give my son his life back. It's a bit impertinent taking up her time, my worries must seem very trivial compared to the important things she has to do. But she won't grudge an old woman. It'll only take her a few minutes, I expect. And after all, I gave her my son when she needed him, so she can give him back now I need him.

NARRATOR. So the old woman left her cat with the neighbours and set out for the court.

> *The* OLD WOMAN *goes out and the* DEAD SOLDIER *on the stretcher is carried out or put upstage.*

THE COURT

NARRATOR. The queen was busy in the palace having great thoughts on behalf of her people.

> *The* QUEEN *comes on singing 'The Camptown Races' and playing with a yo-yo.*

The Prime Minister was granted an audience as he was anxious to compare his great thoughts with hers.

> *The* PM *comes on singing 'A Life on the Ocean Waves' and playing with a yo-yo.*

QUEEN. Good day.
PM. Good day, mam.

QUEEN. Ideal weather for bowling/swimming/running/jumping/ giving a garden party/getting crowned/getting married/making your will/taking in lodgers/lifting up your heart/counting your blessings/or departing this life. Select the word or phrase of your choice and delete the others as appropriate.

PM. Yes, mam.

QUEEN. And how is your wife/mistress/mother/boy friend/dog/ aunt/son/pet alligator/lady love/fancy man/little bit on the side/ the old other/your Saturday night grunt and grind? Take appropriate as already indicated.

PM. Woof-woof is fine, mam.

QUEEN. And would you like a drink/tea/coffee/health beverage/ cocoa/cigarette/smoke/twist/roll/wad/fix/or burn?

PM. I'll have whatever your majesty's having, mam.

QUEEN. Yes. (*Slight pause.*) I see. (*Slight pause.*) Well in that case, I'm having something/nothing/a little/a lot/just a drop/I'm fasting this week/help yourself/never touch the stuff/after you.

PM. That's just what I fancied.

QUEEN. Well, I'm delighted/shattered/crestfallen/woebegone/ elated/filled with foreboding/bowled out/seriously perturbed/ hysterical/and totally indifferent to everything you say.

NARRATOR. The conversation meandered on in this pleasant and well-bred way for three days and then the Prime Minister mentioned why he'd come.

PM. I have a problem.

QUEEN. O dear/tut tut/dearie me/whatever next/lawksa muckey/ always safe in your hands/thank God I bank abroad/my duty is to serve/not a glimmer showed on her marble brow.

PM. No, mam, your majesty doesn't understand.

QUEEN. Nonsense! I understand everything except dirty jokes.

PM. I meant I hadn't made myself clear, mam.

QUEEN. That obviously would be a formidable task.

PM. An old woman's come to court. Her son was a soldier –

QUEEN. Hup/hup/salute/salt of the earth/last bastion/noble mind in a noble body/fire on the count of three.

PM. – who was killed –

QUEEN. Dearly beloved/half a minute's silence/honoured dust/
gave his all/heard the summons/history is written in blood.

PM. And now she wants him back.

QUEEN. I see. Her faith in the monarchy is certainly touching.
Well as it happens I've done all the resurrections I intend to do
this week, so instead I shall offer her something. Would she like
a drink/tea/coffee/health beverage/cocoa/cigarette –

PM. I think I know someone who could help us. He's a very
clever man. Knows everything. Comes from Oxford – or Cam-
bridge – or Sussex – or somewhere. Anyway, he's been taught to
play with two yo-yos!

QUEEN. Two! Let him in.

PM. I shall set him a test for your majesty to see. I've written our
problem on this card.

> The PM *takes out a card, beckons off stage, the* MAGICIAN
> *hurries on, and the* PM *hands him the card.*

PM. Read this and give your answer in sixty seconds.

MAGICIAN (*looks at the card. Immediately*). Eureka! The old
woman can't have her son back because you still need him. He's
being turned into bronze and will stand in the main square to
remind us of all the young men our enemy's killed. Would your
majesty care to unveil him?

QUEEN. What a clever/wonderful/stupid/boring/dazzling/wet/
happy/disgraceful/infantile/sublime/uninteresting idea.

PM. Thank you, mam.

QUEEN. Have you any more ideas? You wouldn't know what's
going to win the four o'clock?

MAGICIAN. No. But I've invented a bomb with a bang twice as
loud as anyone else's. I propose to drop it on our enemy.

QUEEN. How nice/charming/amusing/crude/fascinating/silly/vul-
gar/narrowminded/mean spirited/and dull. Well. it's a pity
about the four o'clock but I can see you're still a great asset to

any government and I needn't waste words on that! Tell me about yourself? Have you a family?

MAGICIAN. I did have but they left me. I don't know why. All except my son – he was one and a half and too little to walk. But he's gone too now. I had to go out one day to give a lecture to my students. I left him playing happily on the mat in front of the fire and I gave him a box of matches, a loaded machine gun, several large plastic bags and an open razor to amuse himself with. When I came back from the lecture – which was called Science and the Responsible Citizen and which by the way was a great success – I found the little chap had had an accident. Robin or William or Charles, or whatever it was I'd christened him, was dead. But one feels that being so clumsy he would not have grown up to be a scientist anyway –

QUEEN. O dear/tut tut/dearie me/lackaday and woe alas.

MAGICIAN. – so I'm resigned to my loss.

QUEEN. What a noble sentiment! Nobility of mind always makes me so pleased/moved/stirred/frigid/relaxed –

PM (*interrupting*). Shall we unveil the monument and drop the bomb now?

QUEEN. – elevated/bored/reduced to tears/yawn/scream/overflow/faint/drop off/ button up/lose myself in flower arranging –

They all go out, the QUEEN *still talking.*

THE MONUMENT ON A LAUNCHING PAD

The Monument stands behind the players throughout the play. Till it's unveiled, in this scene, it's covered with a large white sheet. The OLD WOMAN *comes on and looks at the monument. There is also a small stand with two buttons on it.*

OLD WOMAN. What a great day in our lives! Who would have

thought that my son, born in a very simple home, would one day be so honoured?

The QUEEN, PM *and* MAGICIAN *come on from the direction opposite to the way they left. The* QUEEN *wears a large hat and carries a large handbag. She is still talking.*

QUEEN. – shout hallelujah/retire to Elba/sign the pledge/take up crochet work/or emigrate to Australia.

A LITTLE GIRL (*or* SKINNY, ANGULAR SCHOOL MISTRESS) *steps forward with a bunch of flowers. She hesitates in confusion and then decides – she goes to the* PM, *bobs, and hands him the flowers. He hits her once or twice with the flowers, shoves them back in her hand and pushes her across to the* QUEEN. *The* LITTLE GIRL *bobs again and holds out the flowers. The* QUEEN *smiles and takes them.*

QUEEN. What lovely blooms! Aren't they pretty/bright/colourful/exotic/well arranged/red/blue/my favourites/nice/nasty/bad for hay-fever/good for asthma/cheering.

While the QUEEN *speaks the* LITTLE GIRL *mimes grotesque shyness. Now she stands on one leg, bobs, almost falls over, starts to cry and runs out. The* PM *takes the* QUEEN *to the small stand.*

PM. This is the monument, mam, and here we have two buttons. That one drops the bomb and that one unveils the monument. I suggest we drop the bomb first and then that will be out of the way.

QUEEN. I see. Now which button is which again? I don't want to get it wrong.

PM (*points*). That's for the bomb.

QUEEN. Yes, well there are two of them and that's very confusing. However, I will make an effort and do what I can. Now I'll just say a few words. (*She hands the flowers to the* PM, *takes a sheet of paper from her handbag, and reads from it very exactly.*) Yakety-yakety-yak-yak, yo-ho-ho and yoo-hoo-hoo.

PM. Hear, hear.

QUEEN. Furthermore. Bla-bla-bla, hands, knees and boo-see-daisy, hickery-dickery-dock.

PM. Amen.

QUEEN. Thank you. Not only that but also bla-bla-bla, one small step for mankind, hey-diddle-diddle, I wonder what we're having for dinner, ba-ba, moo-moo, cheep-cheep, and quack-quack!

PM. Well put.

QUEEN. It now gives me great pleasure to press this button and may God bless all who sail in her. (*Slight pause.*) Prime Minister, did you tell me which button was which? I don't want to press the wrong button.

PM. Press *that* one, mam.

QUEEN. That one. Well, it *is* very confusing but I think I can remember that for five seconds if I empty my mind and stop wondering what won the five-thirty. So let's have another try. And may God bless all who sail in her. (*She presses the button. A moment's pause. She looks round.*) Shouldn't something have happened? Oh, I see what it is: I forgot to lift my finger off the button. Prime Minister, why didn't you remind me that would be necessary? O dear. Now it's stuck. (*Loudly to the audience.*) There'll be a slight – (*She pulls her finger.*) – but it's all right. (*To* PM.) The hole's a shade too small for my – (*Loudly to audience.*) Don't panic, it's all under control. My finger is stuck. In the hole. We won't keep you a moment. (*Still trying to pull her finger out.*) Talk amongst yourselves – or hum a little tune. (*Furiously to* PM.) Do something! Don't stand there twitching! I'll change the government. (*Loudly to audience.*) Are you having a nice time? I'll be with you soon. It's my finger. I depressed the button and because my finger is stuck the button is now unable to return to its correct position and consequently – (*To* PM.) Do something! My arm's going dead! (*Loudly to audience.*) Perhaps someone would like to tell us an amusing story?

PM (*hitting* MAGICIAN *with the flowers*). Do something! Do something! I know who put you up to this! The bounder! It's a socialistic plot!

QUEEN. I'm going to faint.

MAGICIAN (*pulling her arm*). There's nothing wrong with the hole! You press too hard.

QUEEN (*hitting him with her handbag*). I spend my life pressing buttons! I know when a button's pressed and when it isn't! (*Yells.*) Ow! You're pulling my arm off!

PM (*cries and hits the* MAGICIAN *with the flowers*). You'll get me sacked! I'll lose my lovely job!

MAGICIAN (*still pulling*). Her finger's too big!

QUEEN. There's nothing wrong with my finger; it's your hole!

> *The finger suddenly comes out. There is the sound of a great rushing wind as the bomb is sent off. The three wave after it.*

MAGICIAN. It works! My bomb works!

PM. Hip hip hooray! Hip hip hooray! Hip hip hooray!

QUEEN. Bon voyage/send us a postcard/don't drink water from the tap/be kind to the froggies, remember they haven't had our advantages. (*Sighs.*) Well, that's that. (*The* PM *and* MAGICIAN *shake hands and laugh.*) Now, let's finish our other little chore. I hope there's nothing wrong with this button –

MAGICIAN. There was nothing wrong with the other one –

> *The* QUEEN *hits him with her handbag and the* PM *hits him with the flowers.*

QUEEN. Shut up! – because if there is I'll suspend your grant and you'll spend the rest of your academic life working on a cure for the common cold. Well, you've been warned. Now, where's my speech? (*She searches in her handbag, takes out a sheet of paper and reads.*) Dear Bootykins, I was on sentry go last night and as, by a lucky mischance, my sentry box is under your window, when you was switching on the electric light I saw – No, that's from a friend of mine, a dear, comical, whimsical fellow, though I can never get him to wipe his feet when he calls. (*Takes another paper from her bag.*) One sliced loaf, one jar of Oxford marmalade – No. (*Takes another paper from her bag.*) List of suspects to be followed by my dear husband in plain clothes. No. It's here somewhere. (*Searching in bag.*) Green Shield stamps. No. Little Black Book. No. Big Black Book. No. Here it is! (*She takes out a paper and reads.*) The Monument, a poem by our Poet Laureate.

> This monument is very nice
> It stands so still in wind and ice
> And never frowns or makes a cry
> Just stares ahead into the sky
> It does what all good people should
> That's why I think it's very good.

Well, I don't know that that was worth looking for, though the sentiment is, of course, admirable. Still, I must have a word with someone about him. Now, I have great pleasure in declaring this monument open.

The wind has died down to a low, sinister howl. The QUEEN *presses the button and the white sheet falls. There is a full-size cross and on it is nailed and bound a crucified pig. A soldier's helmet is nailed over its head. (The pig is to be obtained from a slaughter house and not killed for the performance.) The* QUEEN, PM *and* MAGICIAN *salute. The National Anthem is played in the Elgar version.*

OLD WOMAN. That doesn't look very like my son. But then I haven't seen him naked since he was a child. I don't recognize his hands, but of course they've made him into a soldier and taught him to hold a rifle so his hands are bound to be changed. And now I look I do see my son's face – and his mouth – and his eyes. He was such a quiet, kind, inward boy. He seemed to suffer such a lot and I could never really help him. Yes, I know him now. That's him. I can see the old suffering in his face. My poor child! I'm glad I live in the country and not in this city. I couldn't walk by him and look at his face every day. It's opened my heart and my eyes must be full of tears. Dear, dear. I must go away. I must go away.

The wind has faded almost into silence.

NARRATOR. Unfortunately the enemy king had a magician who was cleverer than the Queen's magician, and he could play with three yo-yos. When the enemy saw the queen's bomb coming towards them they fired their own bomb, and that was even bigger.

An explosion. Light. Noise. Smoke. Movement. The people onstage run round in panic.

PM. Help!

QUEEN. I'm lost!

MAGICIAN. Carambe! What a bomb! How did he do that? I must find out! Where are my books? My microscope? My electroscope? My telescope? Where's my laboratory? Can anyone see my test tubes? Don't tread on my test tubes! Where are my animals? Where are my cages?

QUEEN. I'm lost! Where's my palace? Where's my robe? I've lost my crown! Has anyone seen my crown? Who's taken my throne? It's all lost!

PM. I'm lost! Where are my files? My reports? I can't find any documents! What's burning? Are my despatches burning? I'm lost!

OLD WOMAN. O dear! Where is the city? What's become of it? It was here and now it's gone! Just like that! Where are all the people? They've all gone! I'm lost!

NARRATOR. There was nothing left. Everything was burned or broken and blown away. There was only a storm of dust and a howling wind. They could hear dogs yelping in the ruins but they could never catch one to eat. They wandered about for days, round and round and on and on, and they got hungrier and more tired and unhappy. They were lost.

THE WILDERNESS

While the Narrator has been speaking the QUEEN, OLD WOMAN, PM *and* MAGICIAN *have been wandering round the stage. Now the* QUEEN *sits.*

QUEEN. I've come to the end. Prime Minister, this is a crisis. Do something.

PM. The matter is receiving my urgent attention/being completely ignored/is under review/has got out of hand/is being left over/awaiting developments/totally beyond my very limited capacities.

QUEEN. He's gone mad. (*To the* MAGICIAN.) You do something!

MAGICIAN. I'm examining the dust. I'm taking specimens of dust from everything. I have the dust of trees. This is the dust of rocks. The dust of earth. This must be the dust of clothes. The dust of men. The dust of birds. I've even got the dust of sand. I'll soon be on to something. The answer lies in dust. Dust will save us. I'm wrestling with it and soon it will yield up its secrets to my relentless, probing mind.

NARRATOR. Just then a bird began to sing joyfully. It was the first happy sound they'd heard since the bomb fell on them. They looked up and saw Christ and Buddha coming towards them over the ruined fields.

CHRIST *comes in supported by* BUDDHA. CHRIST *wears a robe and* BUDDHA *a loin cloth.*

QUEEN. Haven't we met somewhere? I don't know that strange, swarthy fellow – though I may have bumped into him when I was running around the colonies, only they all look alike – but I know you . . . Now I know! We're from the same family, almost. Howdyoudo. (*She shakes his hand.*) I suppose the Almighty sent you. Why couldn't he come himself? Well, you're here now – not before time. You know I've lost my crown and my palace – everything. I suppose you've come to get them back for me.

CHRIST. I'm sorry, I can't stop now.

QUEEN. What? Don't you realize how urgent this is?

CHRIST. This is Easter and I'm going to be crucified.

BUDDHA. It's a long way to go. He's tired and I'm helping him so that he has enough strength to die properly when he gets there.

CHRIST. Yes, my friend, thank you for your compassion. We've come a long way and there will be only suffering and bitterness at the end. But you help me. When I feel your arm holding me I don't mind the stones and dust so much, and when I die I shall look at your smile and be at peace. But we must go on quickly. Everywhere children are crying, mothers and fathers are groaning, and old men and women are shrieking as if they were mad. All the animals are broken and bleeding. I must die soon so that the world can be healed. When I have dived to the bottom of the sea all this suffering will end.

BUDDHA. Look, my brother, isn't this your cross? Surely we're here.

CHRIST *goes to the foot of the cross and looks up at the crucified pig.*

CHRIST. I am too late. I can't be crucified for men because they've already crucified themselves, wasted their lives in misery, destroyed their homes and run like madmen over the fields stamping on the animals and plants and everything that lived. They've lost their hope, destroyed their happiness, forgotten mercy and kindness and turned love into suspicion and hate. Their cleverness has become cunning, their skill has become jugglery, their risks have become reckless gambles, they are mad. How can I suffer for men, what are my sufferings compared to theirs? How can one innocent die for the guilty when so many innocents are corrupted and killed? This is a hell worse than anything my father imagined.

BUDDHA. Cry and I'll wipe your tears and lead you somewhere else. Lean on me. We'll find another world where they'll accept our priceless gift of peace.

CHRIST. But where? This is our place. There was to be love and kindness and good sense here. There was to be peace.

MAGICIAN. I have it! I have it! I'm sure my figures are right! Yes! I can make a bomb out of dust! We're saved!

QUEEN. Is this true? Has God answered my prayers? Hurrah! I'll give you a medal! All my medals!

PM. I knew we'd bounce back. We land on our feet. You can't sink the island race. I'll scout round and muster up a few soldiers, there must be a few men or women and children left – we all serve when the hour sounds.

BUDDHA. You see they are mad. They have no pity. They can't pity each other, so how could they ever listen to us?

QUEEN. My strength's returning! I shall make a speech. (*She clears her throat.*) People advance! Forward/onward/backward/ ladies and infants to the side/over the hills/into the blue/the horizon beyond the dust/sound of the trumpet/up and down and on . . .

CHRIST *and* BUDDHA *have gone out quickly while the* QUEEN *talks. Now the* QUEEN, PM *and* MAGICIAN *go out quickly.*

PM (*going*). Hear hear!

MAGICIAN (*going*). Caramba!

NARRATOR. It was at this moment that the old woman found the body of her son. It had been blown out of its grave. She lifted him up by the shoulders and rested him against her and as she did so he seemed to speak. It was only gas escaping from his decaying belly and passing out through his teeth, but he seemed to say this –

The OLD WOMAN *has sat the* DEAD SOLDIER *up. We hear him speak.*

A DEAD SOLDIER'S THOUGHTS

My tanks set fire to corn
My bullets stripped trees
I made where I was a grave
And walked and laughed in it
Once in a little quiet
I watched a singing bird
Build a nest
In the cardboard boxes we used to put bodies in

My flares blind stars
My guns shatter thunder
I ravaged more than plagues and famine
My bayonet was sharp
Whetted on blood and cries of unpitied men
I crippled to make men happy
Built prisons to set them free
The simpleton drooling in a bath-chair inherited under my will
I am the father of millions of orphans

I am dead
The bird sang
When blood ran out of my arms
It sings still
I lie in my grave and it has the sky
If I could rise now on wings and fly
I would sing
I would sing

Madmen, peace!
You who bend iron but are afraid of grass
Peace!

The dust on my wings shines in the sun
I have learned to sing in winter and dance in my shroud
I have learned that a pig is a form of lamb
And power is impotence
Madmen, you are the fallen!

Methuen's Modern Plays

EDITED BY JOHN CULLEN AND GEOFFREY STRACHAN

Paul Ableman	*Green Julia*
Jean Anouilh	*Antigone*
	Becket
	Poor Bitos
	Ring Round the Moon
	The Lark
	The Fighting Cock
	Dear Antoine
	The Director of the Opera
John Arden	*Serjeant Musgrave's Dance*
	The Workhouse Donkey
	Armstrong's Last Goodnight
	Left-Handed Liberty
	Soldier, Soldier and other plays
	Two Autobiographical Plays
John Arden and	*The Business of Good Government*
Margaretta d'Arcy	*The Royal Pardon*
	The Hero Rises Up
	The Island of the Mighty
Ayckbourn, Bowen, Brook, Campton, Melly, Owen, Pinter, Saunders, Weldon	*Mixed Doubles*
Brendan Behan	*The Quare Fellow*
	The Hostage
	Richard's Cork Leg
Edward Bond	*Saved*
	Narrow Road to the Deep North
	The Pope's Wedding
	Lear
	The Sea
	Bingo
John Bowen	*Little Boxes*
	The Disorderly Women

Joe Orton	*Crimes of Passion*
	Loot
	What the Butler Saw
	Funeral Games and The Good and Faithful Servant
	Entertaining Mr Sloane
Harold Pinter	*The Birthday Party*
	The Room and The Dumb Waiter
	The Caretaker
	A Slight Ache and other plays
	The Collection and The Lover
	The Homecoming
	Tea Party and other plays
	Landscape and Silence
	Old Times
	No Man's Land
David Selbourne	*The Damned*
Jean-Paul Sartre	*Crime Passionnel*
Wole Soyinka	*Madmen and Specialists*
	Death and the King's Horseman
	The Jero Plays
Theatre Workshop and Charles Chilton	*Oh What a Lovely War*
Boris Vian	*The Empire Builders*
Peter Weiss	*Trotsky in Exile*
Charles Wood	*'H'*
	Veterans
Carl Zuckmayer	*The Captain of Köpenick*

If you would like regular information on new Methuen plays and theatre books, please write to:

The Marketing Department
Eyre Methuen Ltd
North Way
Andover
Hants